'YOU CAN'T WIN ANYTHING WITH KIDS'

'YOU CAN'T WIN ANYTHING WITH KIDS'

A HISTORY OF THE ENGLISH PREMIER LEAGUE TOLD THROUGH QUOTES

GAVIN NEWSHAM

FOREWORD BY GARY NEVILLE

B L O O M S B U R Y

LONDON · OXFORD · NEW YORK · NEW DELHI · SYDNEY

Bloomsbury Sport
An imprint of Bloomsbury Publishing Plc

50 Bedford Square	1385 Broadway
London	New York
WC1B 3DP	NY 10018
UK	USA

www.bloomsbury.com

BLOOMSBURY and the Diana logo are trademarks of Bloomsbury Publishing Plc

First published in 2017
Text © Gavin Newsham, 2017

British Library Cataloguing-in-Publication Data
A catalogue record for this book is available from the British Library.

ISBN: Hardback: 9781472946935
ePub: 9781472946928
ePDF: 9781472946911

2 4 6 8 10 9 7 5 3 1

Typeset in Adobe Caslon by Deanta Global Publishing Services, Chennai, India
Printed and bound in Great Britain by CPI Group (UK) Ltd. Croydon , CR0 4YY

To find out more about our authors and books visit www.bloomsbury.com.
Here you will find extracts, author interviews, details of forthcoming events and the option to sign up for our newsletters.

Contents

Foreword by Gary Neville

It does seem like a very long time ago that I made my Premier League debut for United. It was on the final day of the 1993/94 season when we faced Coventry City at Old Trafford. We had already won the title and I, a fresh-faced 19-year-old, was given a chance in defence alongside Steve Bruce, Gary Pallister and Denis Irwin. We kept a clean sheet that day but it ended up goalless. Hardly a match to remember. But I was lucky. I was lucky to play 400 times in the top-flight. Lucky to have some world-class players as friends and team-mates. And lucky to play under the greatest manager of the modern era. But, more than that, I was lucky to play in what was, and remains, the greatest league in the world: the Premier League. It's been 25 years since the Premier League began and it's a competition that never ceases to amaze me. On one hand, it's ushered in a new era of professionalism and helped introduce a rich wave of talent from around the world to our shores. On the other, it's taken the English game to every corner of the planet. It's always fascinating, never predictable. Look at Leicester City and what they achieved in 2015/16; you just can't write that kind of script. And it will be the same next year. Records will be broken, new stars will emerge and many more memories made. Long it may last. Enjoy the book.

Gary Neville

Introduction

Saturday 15 August 1992. It's a landmark day in football, and not just because Norwich enjoyed a rare win at Arsenal or Sheffield United managed to beat Manchester United. No, this is the day, the momentous day, that English football changed forever – the day the FA Premier League was born.

To date, a total of 47 clubs have taken part in the Premier League since its inception. Just six teams (Arsenal, Chelsea, Everton, Liverpool, Manchester United and Tottenham Hotspur) have been ever-present, while some clubs, like Cardiff, Barnsley, Blackpool and Swindon, have dipped their toes into the Premier League for one season only, never to return.

But whether your team is challenging for trophies at the top of the table or striving just to reach the promised land, there can be no denying that the Premier League has changed the very face of football in England (and much further afield), initiating the kind of advances that might not have happened had the status quo remained in place.

Take a cursory glance at the league as it is today and you'll see stadiums and facilities that are not just better, but pretty much full, week in, week out; the playing surfaces have moved from quagmires to bowling greens; and the players, thanks in no small part to an influx of foreign coaches with new ideas and innovations, are quicker, technically better and significantly more athletic.

And, of course, it's managed to spark some truly extraordinary stories over its rich history. Remember Kevin Keegan's on-air meltdown? Or Paolo Di Canio's shove on referee Paul Alcock? How about those jaw-on-the-floor goals like Tony Yeboah's volley for Leeds against Liverpool or Sergio Aguero's last-gasp title-winning goal for Manchester City? And what about some of those wonderful teams that played some wondrous football, like all-conquering Manchester United and Arsenal's fabled 'Invincibles'?

It's moments like these that have propelled the Premier League into hitherto unseen levels of popularity. Today, a quarter of a century since it came into being, the competition is so huge that its appeal stretches to virtually every part of the planet, with the broadcasting rights to show live games sold everywhere from Australia to China, from Singapore to sub-Saharan Africa, and its players as popular in Bangkok as they are in Birmingham.

And that's exactly what we've tried to capture in '*You Can't Win Anything With Kids*'. Using the thoughts, views, words and wisdom of the managers, players and fans who have lived through the Premier League era, it's an attempt to jog some memories as well as relive all those memorable moments, be they dazzling, infamous or simply unbearable.

It's also the perfect opportunity to enjoy some of the funniest, most insightful and sometimes perplexing soundbites from the last 25 years, whether it be the endlessly amusing spat between José Mourinho and Arsène Wenger, Eric Cantona's deeply philosophical musings or Joe Kinnear's foul-mouthed ones.

And yes, we will mention Alan Hansen…

PREMIER LEAGUE 1992/93

A Whole New Ball Game

It's a new dawn for English football, a big bang moment that will change the domestic game forever.

Following the breakaway of the 22 leading clubs from the Football League on 27 May 1992, a new organisation, the FA Premier League, and their new competition, the Premiership, kicks off in August 1992 with 22 teams taking part, namely Arsenal, Aston Villa, Blackburn Rovers, Chelsea, Coventry City, Crystal Palace, Everton, Ipswich Town, Leeds United, Liverpool, Manchester City, Manchester United, Middlesbrough, Norwich City, Nottingham Forest, Oldham Athletic, Queens Park Rangers, Sheffield United, Sheffield Wednesday, Southampton, Tottenham Hotspur and Wimbledon.

Overnight, the league becomes one of the most attractive, high-profile sports contests in the world, not least because it's backed by a massive £305 million live television deal with BSkyB (and the BBC for match highlights). With more coverage than ever before, the clubs cash in, gaining lucrative new sponsorship deals and with many floating on the stock market. The players benefit too. Salaries rise significantly, as do transfer fees. It is, as the BSkyB slogan maintains, 'a whole new ball game'.

A case in point is newly promoted Blackburn Rovers. Backed by the personal fortune of steel magnate Jack Walker, they signal their intent by breaking the British transfer record in the close season, paying £3.6 million for Southampton's 21-year-old striker Alan Shearer.

The inaugural Premier League season starts on Saturday 15 August and it takes just five minutes for the first goal of the new era to be scored. The honour goes to Sheffield United striker Brian Deane, who heads home Alan Cork's flick-on to give the Blades the lead. They go on to win the game 2-1.

"It is good to look back on … Anybody would be happy to be the first scorer."

Brian Deane recalls his most famous goal.[1]

....

There's a shock result at Highbury, too, as Arsenal let slip a two-goal lead to lose 4-2 to Norwich City. The man that makes the difference is Mark Robins, who signed from Manchester United in the close season, and who scores two brilliantly taken goals.

> **"New boy [Mark] shows the speed of thought and instinct of all great goalscorers."**
>
> Tony Gubba, BBC *Match of the Day* commentator[2]

....

It's a successful debut for Blackburn's record signing Alan Shearer, too. He scores twice in a 3-3 draw with Crystal Palace.

> **"You obviously need good players in every position but you need goals and he [Shearer] was a world-class player."**
>
> Colin Hendry, Blackburn defender[3]

....

The following day sees BSkyB televise their first live Premier League game as they cover Nottingham Forest's home game against Liverpool. The programme is hosted by Richard Keys, with former Everton and Scotland striker Andy Gray accompanying Martin Tyler in the commentary box, and is memorable for a stunning winner by Teddy Sheringham.

"I called Teddy's goal 'a peach', it's a word I've hardly used since. It was worthy of winning the first live game – a super goal past David James in the Liverpool net."

Martin Tyler, Sky Sports commentator[4]

On 19 September, Liverpool's Ronny Rosenthal makes his mark in Premier League history – for all the wrong reasons. The Reds are away at Aston Villa when the Israeli striker seizes on a long punt forward from his goalkeeper, David James. He shimmies around Villa keeper Nigel Spink, takes a touch and steadies himself. Then, just 10 yards out from an open goal, he shoots – and somehow hits the crossbar. Ironically, Rosenthal actually scores that day, although Liverpool still lost 4-2. But nobody remembers that goal.

> **"Does it bother me? No, it doesn't matter now. I'm glad it happened! I'm glad I missed because I'm still on the map [because of it]."**
>
> Ronny Rosenthal[5]

Defending champions Leeds United make an indifferent start to their defence, winning just twice in the first 10 games. There are some crumbs of comfort, though, as their French striker Eric Cantona scores six times in a four-game streak, including a hat trick in a 5-0 win over Spurs.

But in a shock development, his time at Elland Road comes to a surprise end on 26 November as he makes a £1.2 million move to Manchester United. Though Leeds are happy to offload a player notorious for his unpredictable behaviour, it will turn out to be one of the biggest coups in the history of the Premier League.

> **"Leaving a club is like leaving a woman. When there's nothing left to say, you go."**
>
> Eric Cantona[6]

It's a view reinforced by Everton manager Howard Kendall.

> **"I made a number of enquiries and everyone said the same thing: 'He's totally unsuitable for English football.' Needless to say, I acted on that information and turned him down."**
>
> Howard Kendall, on why he rejected Eric Cantona.[7]

And yet it might never have happened. Originally, Alex Ferguson was intent on buying David Hirst from Sheffield Wednesday but got no response from their manager, Trevor Francis. That's when he turned to Cantona.

The temperamental French star would make an immediate impact at Old Trafford. United embark on a nine-game unbeaten run, winning seven, and the Frenchman scores four times.

> "Eric Cantona is so clever it's untrue and the lovely thing about special players is they're infectious. The things he tries, the others try, and it's the way the team are playing that's got middle-aged fans jumping about like two-year-olds."
>
> Alex Ferguson, Manchester United manager[8]

Come December and it was Norwich City that were the unlikely leaders of the Premier League, and this despite having a negative goal difference. And therein lay their problem. Though the Canaries were often a force of nature going forward, they were shaky beyond belief at the back, a 7-1 defeat at Blackburn and a 4-1 reverse at Liverpool being cases in point.

A 1-0 defeat at Old Trafford on 12 December would burst the balloon on their surprising progress. Mike Walker's team would take just three points from their next six games until a 4-2 win over Crystal Palace stopped the rot.

But the dip in form allows Norwich to be overtaken by Aston Villa and Manchester United. Villa's surge up the table is inspired by the new attack of Dean Saunders and Dalian Atkinson and it's the latter's dazzling solo run and deft chip against Wimbledon that wins the Goal of the Season award.

"He scored spectacular goals. He didn't get many tap-ins. I think that one against Wimbledon is the one everybody remembers him for, though."

Ron Atkinson, Aston Villa manager in the 1992/93 season. Tragically, Dalian Atkinson died in 2016 after being tasered by police. He was 48.[9]

Dalian Atkinson's form was already good before Dean Saunders signed. After the Welshman arrives, it gets even better. He scores 11 goals in the first 19 games of the season, including the only goal in Villa's home win over Manchester United. But a muscle injury would sideline Atkinson for two-and-a-half months and with their star striker out of their side, Villa's title charge would falter.

"If he hadn't got injured I think we would have won the league because him and Dean were the best strikeforce in the Premier League."

Ron Atkinson, Aston Villa manager[10]

Atkinson isn't the only in-form striker to be sidelined, as Blackburn's title challenge is undone by a snapped anterior cruciate ligament in Alan Shearer's right knee during a game against Leeds United. The England striker has scored 16 goals in 21 games for Rovers but the injury rules him out for the rest of the season.

After 22 matches, it's Manchester United that hold the narrowest of advantages over Aston Villa, leading by goal difference. Against Sheffield Wednesday at Hillsborough they storm back from three goals down to draw 3-3 and it's a result that, according to Alex Ferguson, augurs well for the rest of the season.

"More than at any time since I was playing, the club is alive. The 3-3 draw at Sheffield Wednesday was magnificent. It's as if the good old days were back."

Alex Ferguson, Manchester United manager[11]

Villa and United vie for the lead throughout the winter. Ron Atkinson's side demolish Middlesbrough 5-1 and beat Liverpool, Chelsea and Everton as they lose just twice in 13 games. With six games to spare, they lead the league but the momentum soon shifts to Manchester United.

In the last five weeks of the season, they win all seven of their remaining games. The key match, however, is the return game against Sheffield Wednesday at Old Trafford on 10 April. A goal down with just minutes remaining, United snatch all three points as Steve Bruce scores in the 86th minute and then again in the 96th minute. United, thanks to what people are now calling 'Fergie Time', have one hand on the trophy.

"It's amazing how clearly everyone remembers that game and the late goals and the amount of injury time which was played …"

Steve Bruce, Manchester United's two-goal hero[12]

> "[Chris] Waddle asked me if Mickey Mouse had fallen off my watch, which gives you an idea of what it was like. I was questioned, certainly, but it was all good natured."
>
> Match referee John Hilditch on the 'Fergie Time' that helped United win.[13]

There's despair at Nottingham Forest where Brian Clough, the legendary manager who took the club from the old Second Division and on to the title and back-to-back European Cup wins, calls time on his 18-year reign at the City Ground in the most heartbreaking fashion. Forest lose 10 of their last 14 matches to finish bottom of the table, ending a 16-year stay in the top flight.

> *"Can't avoid the truth. Can't make it look better than it is. Only one thing to be said. We're in the s***."*
>
> The one, the only Brian Clough.[14]

> "Only Brian Clough could perform a lap of honour on the day his team dropped out of the Premiership..."
>
> Pat Murphy, *The Guardian*[15]

Aston Villa's title race is run on Sunday 2 May, when relegation-threatened Oldham Athletic pull off a shock victory at Villa Park, winning 1-0 thanks to a Nick Henry goal. The defeat hands the title to Manchester United and Alex Ferguson learns of the news as he's playing golf with his son Mark at Mottram Hall in Cheshire.

"I looked up to the 17th green and saw him. So I stopped the car and climbed up to the raised green and, apparently in a very polite manner, told him the good news. First of all, he did a double take because he wanted to make sure I wasn't taking the mickey. As soon as he was satisfied with that, he just went absolutely crazy."

Michael Lavender, the stranger who told Alex Ferguson that Manchester United were champions.[16]

As United celebrated, Oldham Athletic continued with their bid to pull off one of the greatest escapes. Bottom of the table with 10 games to play, the Latics had gone into their final three games – the Villa game being the first – needing to win all three to have any chance of staying up.

Incredibly, they do it. Three days after the win over Villa, Joe Royle's side beat Liverpool 3-2, while on the final day of the season they hold on to win 4-3 against Southampton. When Crystal Palace lose 3-0 at Arsenal on the same day, it means that Palace are relegated on goal difference.

"There have been a lot of shredded nerves and some games have aged me five years. But it's great for us and we've deserved it. We always have a go, we try to score goals."

Joe Royle, Oldham's relieved manager.[17]

The following day, Manchester United take the plaudits in their penultimate game against Blackburn Rovers at Old Trafford. Leading 2-1 going into injury time, United call upon the only player in their side who hasn't scored in the season, defender Gary Pallister, to take a free kick 20 yards out from the Rovers goal. Fittingly, he steps up and drills the ball right into the corner.

> *"This is the greatest achievement, the greatest moment of my football career. I couldn't have asked for anything else."*
>
> United manager, Alex Ferguson[18]

The wait is over.

Manchester United, after 26 long years, are champions of England once more.

Games Played: 42

Pos	Team	GD	Pts
1	Manchester United	+36	84
2	Aston Villa	+17	74
3	Norwich City	-4	72
4	Blackburn Rovers	+22	71
5	Queens Park Rangers	+8	63
6	Liverpool	+7	59
7	Sheffield Wednesday	+4	59
8	Tottenham Hotspur	-6	59
9	Manchester City	+5	57
10	Arsenal	+2	56
11	Chelsea	-3	56
12	Wimbledon	+1	54
13	Everton	-2	53
14	Sheffield United	+1	52
15	Coventry City	-5	52
16	Ipswich Town	-5	52
17	Leeds United	-5	51
18	Southampton	-7	50
19	Oldham Athletic	-11	49
20	Crystal Palace	-13	49
21	Middlesbrough	-21	44
22	Nottingham Forest	-21	40

CHAMPIONS: Manchester United

RUNNERS-UP: Aston Villa

RELEGATED: Crystal Palace, Middlesbrough, Nottingham Forest

PROMOTED: Newcastle United, West Ham United, Swindon Town

TOP GOALSCORER: Teddy Sheringham, Nottingham Forest and Tottenham Hotspur – 22

PLAYER OF THE SEASON: Paul McGrath, Aston Villa

MANAGER OF THE SEASON: Dave Bassett, Sheffield United

DID YOU KNOW? *Only 13 foreign players took part on the opening day of the first Premier League season, while all 22 club managers were British.*

PREMIER LEAGUE 1993/94

From Strength to Strength

The success of the inaugural season of the Premiership saw its first sponsor arrive in time for the 1993/4 season and, from now on, the competition would be called the FA Carling Premiership, thanks to a £12 million injection from the brewers Bass.

"We are delighted to be associated with what has always been recognised as the most fiercely competitive and exciting League in the world."

Simon MacDonald, Bass marketing director[1]

The success of Manchester United, meanwhile, sees the club keen to build on their success from the 1992/3 season, and as Bryan Robson nears the end of his career they sign a natural replacement, the combative young Irishman Roy Keane. He arrives from Nottingham Forest in a British record deal of £3.75 million.

> "Over in Ireland, everybody seems to support United. When I went home to Cork in the summer everyone was pressurising me to sign for them! My family and friends knew that I had already made up my mind but they still hassled me."
>
> Roy Keane explains his decision to move to Old Trafford, even though he was all set to join Blackburn Rovers.[2]

Having been guided to the top flight for the first time in their history, Swindon Town suffer a setback as manager Glenn Hoddle is headhunted by Chelsea in the close season. And how they miss him. It will be 16 games before Swindon, now under Hoddle's assistant John Gorman, record their first win in the Premiership with a narrow 1-0 win over QPR.

> **"I never felt right about leaving Swindon after getting them promoted. There were a lot of players out of contract, I remember saying to Glenn 'whoever the new manager is they are going to be right in it', or words to that effect. It turned out to be me."**
>
> John Gorman, Swindon manager[3]

At the happy end of the table, Manchester United storm into an 11-point lead by the end of October, giving them clear water at the top. It's a United side that's brimming with confidence. With Eric Cantona in full flow, Lee Sharpe scoring freely and a defence marshalled by Steve Bruce and Gary Pallister, they win 13 of their first 15 games. But it's the young Welsh winger Ryan Giggs who really catches the eye.

> **"I remember when I first saw him. He was 13 and he just floated over the ground like a cocker spaniel chasing a piece of silver paper in the wind."**
>
> Alex Ferguson, Manchester United manager[4]

They lose just once, 1-0 against Chelsea at Stamford Bridge. The Blues would also beat them at Old Trafford by the same score, and on both occasions it's striker Gavin Peacock who gets the only goal. The home defeat also signals the end of United's 22-match unbeaten run.

> *"Oh well, all good things have to come to an end ... Maybe it's not a bad thing to happen. A reminder at the right time."*
>
> Alex Ferguson, Manchester United manager[5]

Their only genuine opposition comes from big-spending Blackburn Rovers. Bankrolled by steel millionaire Jack Walker, they introduce a clutch of new signings, including Tim Flowers for £2.4 million (the most expensive goalkeeper in English football), defender Ian Pearce and midfielder David Batty, and win 16 of their 20 games from December to the middle of April.

Kenny Dalglish's side also record their first win over Manchester United in 30 years when two goals from Alan Shearer help cut the Red Devils' lead at the top of the table to just three points.

"And Shearer's free ... and Alan Shearer scores for Blackburn Rovers! The challengers have taken the lead!"

"There's the inevitable outcome! They're off the bench! Shearer strikes again! Two-nil!"

Martin Tyler, Sky Sports commentator[6]

After a dismal start to the season, Everton part company with their manager Howard Kendall in December. It's Kendall's second spell at Goodison, but he resigns with the club lying in 11th and having just lost to Manchester United in the Coca-Cola League Cup.

> **"I thought if he was going to quit he might have gone after the Manchester United match but he didn't. He stayed and he had seemed quite happy."**
>
> Tony Cottee, Everton forward[7]

As Kendall is replaced by the Norwich City manager Mike Walker, it's not long before near neighbours Liverpool make a managerial change too. Out goes Graeme Souness and in comes a member of the fabled Anfield Boot Room, Roy Evans.

> **"It was a job that I felt I had to do. Though I took it at completely the wrong time ... I was blinded by my feelings for Liverpool."**
>
> Graeme Souness[8]

It's Newcastle that are the surprise package of the season. Newly promoted, they recover from losing their opening two games to climb up to third place as the season enters December. The highlight is a 3-0 win over Liverpool at St James' Park with their prolific striker Andy Cole grabbing all three goals.

> **"[It's] the best 45 minutes we have played in my time here. We were 6-0 up at halftime in one Division One game last year but this was the Premiership."**
>
> Kevin Keegan, Newcastle manager[9]

Buoyed by the never-ending stream of goals from Andy Cole, Newcastle finish the season strongly. At one stage, they score 22 goals in a six-game winning streak, with Cole scoring seven times. They end the campaign in third place having scored 82 goals, the highest of any team in the league. Andy Cole, meanwhile, ends as the top flight's highest scorer with a return of 34 goals.

"He has such great elasticity. He has taken the position at the front of the diamond and he has been a diamond."

Newcastle manager Kevin Keegan on his star striker, Andy Cole.[10]

But it's United's title again – and by some distance. Alex Ferguson's side have led from 21 August and mounted an exemplary defence of their title. They end the season on 92 points and retain their title with two games to spare, a 2-1 win at Ipswich being sufficient to carry them over the line.

But Ferguson doesn't rest on his laurels. Within weeks of their second title, the United manager would take an axe to his successful side, calling time on the Old Trafford careers of Steve Bruce, Gary Pallister, Denis Irwin and Bryan Robson.

> *"I had to remember that I was manager of Manchester United, not their father ... Some people might say it is ruthless but it is about loyalty to the club."*
>
> Alex Ferguson, Manchester United manager[11]

It's the relegation battle that occupies most people's attention on the final day and with Swindon already down and Oldham joining them, there are four teams – Everton, Sheffield United, Ipswich and Southampton – all seeking to avoid the final relegation place. It was Everton that were most at risk. They had to win at Wimbledon and trust that the other results went their way.

But as Everton win 3-2 and Southampton and Ipswich draw against West Ham and Blackburn respectively, it's agony for Sheffield United. Their fate is decided in injury time when a last-ditch goal from Chelsea's Mark Stein gives the Blues a 3-2 win and consigns the Blades to relegation. And yet a draw would have been enough to stay up.

"It wasn't a classic match but the passion of it, the way the fans got behind us and what it meant to everybody made it special. In fact, the supportiveness of the fans is my happiest memory."

A relieved Everton manager, Mike Walker[12]

"When you play Russian Roulette, you sometimes get the bullet."

Dave Bassett, Sheffield United manager[13]

The final goal of Leeds' 5-0 win away at Swindon Town on the final day of the season, meanwhile, is the 100th that the Robins concede in the season. It remains a Premier League record to this day.

"I get remembered as the manager of the team who let in 100 goals and that does bug me. If you look at our goals scored, we scored many more goals than most teams do when they go down."

John Gorman, Swindon manager[14]

Games Played: 42

Pos	Team	GD	Pts
1	Manchester United	+42	92
2	Blackburn Rovers	+27	84
3	Newcastle United	+41	77
4	Arsenal	+25	71
5	Leeds United	+26	70
6	Wimbledon	+3	65
7	Sheffield Wednesday	+22	64
8	Liverpool	+4	60
9	Queens Park Rangers	+1	60
10	Aston Villa	-4	57
11	Coventry City	-2	56
12	Norwich City	+4	53
13	West Ham United	-11	52
14	Chelsea	-4	51
15	Tottenham Hotspur	-5	45
16	Manchester City	-11	45
17	Everton	-21	44
18	Southampton	-17	43
19	Ipswich Town	-23	43
20	Sheffield United	-18	42
21	Oldham Athletic	-26	40
22	Swindon Town	-53	30

CHAMPIONS: Manchester United

RUNNERS-UP: Blackburn Rovers

RELEGATED: Sheffield United, Oldham Athletic, Swindon Town

PROMOTED: Nottingham Forest, Crystal Palace, Leicester City

TOP GOALSCORER: Andy Cole, Newcastle United – 34

PLAYER OF THE SEASON: Eric Cantona, Manchester United

MANAGER OF THE SEASON: Alex Ferguson, Manchester United

DID YOU KNOW? *There were a record 19 hat tricks in the 1993/4 Premiership season.*

The Rovers Return

Having gone 26 years without winning a top-flight title, it had seemed as though the new Premier League competition suited Manchester United just fine. Back-to-back championships saw the Red Devils start as overwhelming favourites to make it a hat trick of Premier League titles.

This is also the last season where there would be 22 clubs in the Premier League and to reduce the number of teams in the division there would be four teams relegated and just two promoted from Division One for this season only.

The season begins in spectacular style and the place to be is Sheffield Wednesday's Hillsborough stadium.

Having impressed with Germany in the World Cup Finals in America in the summer, German striker Jurgen Klinsmann leaves Monaco and signs for Tottenham. Renowned for his diving as much as his goal-scoring exploits, the prolific striker grabs the winner on his Premier League debut in a 4-3 victory at Sheffield Wednesday – and then launches into a spectacular dive to celebrate.

"Is there a diving school in London?"

Jurgen Klinsmann defuses the controversy of his signing with a quip at his first press conference.[1]

> **"We were welcomed at Sheffield Wednesday's stadium by all the diving signs – 5.9, 5.8, all that sort of thing – and we were laughing about it. Then [Teddy] Sheringham had the idea. He said: 'If you score today, we'll all dive.' And I said: 'Okay, but we'll do it once.'"**
>
> Jurgen Klinsmann[2]

But it wasn't just the once. In his first six games, Klinsmann scores seven goals and the celebration quickly becomes his new trademark.

Jurgen Klinsmann isn't the only hotshot in the division. In the second round of fixtures, Liverpool beat Arsenal 3-0 at Anfield and it's their 19-year-old striker Robbie Fowler who grabs all three. What's more, he does it in just four minutes and 32 seconds – the fastest hat trick in Premier League history. Soon after, Liverpool fans give him a new nickname – 'God'.

> *"We all knew how good Robbie was but after that hattrick everyone else took notice as well. For a player so young to do that to Arsenal was incredible..."*
>
> John Barnes, Fowler's Liverpool teammate[3]

It's Newcastle United that surge ahead in the early stages of the campaign. They remain unbeaten in their first 11 games before a 2-0 reverse at Old Trafford against Manchester United at the end of October stops their progress in its tracks, allowing Blackburn, on a run of seven wins on the spin, to take their place at the top.

In November, meanwhile, the Arsenal midfielder Paul Merson admits that he's not only an alcoholic but also addicted to cocaine and gambling. He takes a three-month break from the game to seek help.

> **"The biggest issue was that I was so high most of the time, I didn't have a clue who or what I was gambling on, £10,000 on the Eurovision song contest, £5000 on a bowls match on BBC 2, £20,000 on an NFL game."**
>
> Paul Merson reveals just how bad his problems got.[4]

In early January there's shock, surprise and, in some cases, outrage as Newcastle's manager sanctions the sale of their star striker, Andy Cole, to Manchester United. The Old Trafford club pay £6 million for Cole and also give the Magpies the £1 million-rated winger Keith Gillespie, setting a new British record transfer fee totalling £7 million.

"I never thought Newcastle would sell me to another English club …
I wouldn't have gone to any other club than Manchester United …
It's every schoolboy's dream to play at Old Trafford."

United's new record-signing Andy Cole.[5]

> **"Andy Cole will score goals for Manchester United and there
> are times when that will be rammed down my throat. But
> people shouldn't think that there is any more to this than
> pure footballing judgement."**
>
> Kevin Keegan, Newcastle manager[6]

And Andy Cole did score goals. In that first half-season, he scores 12 goals in just 18 games for United, including five in a 9-0 mauling of Ipswich Town, making him the first player in Premier League history to score five goals in a match.

"He gets the ball and scores a goal, Andy Andy Cole …"

United fans have a new chant that is, invariably, correct.[7]

On 25 January, Manchester United travel to south London to play Crystal Palace at Selhurst Park. Second in the table, they have lost just once in their last 16 games. Three minutes into the second half, United's talismanic Frenchman Eric Cantona is given a red card for kicking out at Palace's Richard Shaw. As he leaves the field of play, he responds to taunts from a Palace supporter, 20-year-old Matthew Simmons, and snaps, launching himself at him with a flying kung-fu kick before trying to land a few punches.

> **"Off! Off! Off! It's an early bath for you, Mr Cantona!"**
>
> What Matthew Simmons maintained he had said to Cantona.[8]

Not surprisingly, the Football Association throw the book at Cantona. His punishments range from a club fine of £20,000 and a ban for the rest of the season to an FA sanction of an eight-month ban and a further £10,000 fine. Later, he gets 120 hours' community service. After his sentencing, he calls a press conference and says just one sentence.

> ## "When the seagulls follow the trawler, it is because they think sardines will be thrown into the sea."
>
> Eric Cantona's press conference statement[9]

> ## "If a Frenchman goes on about seagulls, trawlers and sardines, he's called a philosopher. I'd just be called a short Scottish bum talking c***."
>
> Former Manchester United midfielder Gordon Strachan[10]

Another major news story breaks in February as Arsenal manager George Graham is sacked for taking an illegal payment, or 'bung', from the agent Rune Hauge. The Scot maintains his innocence but he is later banned from the game for a year by the Football Association. He leaves after guiding the Gunners to six trophies, including two league titles and the UEFA Cup Winners' Cup.

> ## "Mr. Graham did not act in the best interests of the club."
>
> Arsenal FC statement[11]

> ## "I have made the welfare of Arsenal my sole objective for the eight and a half years I have been the manager and my track record shows my success. Before that I played for Arsenal for seven years and so I can demonstrate more than 15 years of total commitment to the club. The allegations are nonsense."
>
> George Graham[12]

Though there had been moments where Liverpool, Leeds United and Nottingham Forest had all shown the kind of form to suggest they could mount a title challenge, none have the staying power to keep up with Blackburn Rovers and Manchester United.

As the season reaches its conclusion, United manager Alex Ferguson suggests that Blackburn lack the bottle to win the title. After making a series of key saves in Rovers' 1-0 win over Newcastle United in Blackburn's penultimate game, their goalkeeper Tim Flowers responds to Ferguson's criticism.

"Don't talk to me about bottle. Don't talk to me about bottling it, because that is bottle out there. We are going to fight to the death because we have got bottle and we will give exactly what we have given all season, and that's 100 per cent bottle."

Blackburn's Tim Flowers' post-match interview on Sky Sports.[13]

The final day arrives and it's set up perfectly. Blackburn are top of the table with 89 points and a +42 goal difference, while Manchester United are two points behind with a goal difference of +49. A win for Blackburn at Liverpool and it's all over. Anything else and it's up for grabs.

At Upton Park, Manchester United lay siege to the West Ham goal but they miss chance after chance and the game remains at 1-1. Meanwhile, at Anfield, Blackburn have gone 2-1 down as Jamie Redknapp rifles home an injury-time free kick. All United need is a goal and they will be champions.

In the final 20 minutes, United have 18 attempts on goal but find the Hammers' Czech goalkeeper Ludek Miklosko in inspired form and West Ham, improbably, hold on for a 1-1 draw.

"There's two and a half minutes of the English season left and still the outcome of the championship isn't truly settled yet. A goal for Manchester United now would bring them the title you feel ... This is Scholes ... Cole's through ... He's missed it!"

Tony Gubba, BBC *Match of the Day* commentator[14]

"The thing that struck me most about the day was that none of the West Ham players warmed up. We were safe from relegation, we were totally relaxed and there was no tension ... The only person that warmed up was Ludo – and it showed because he was phenomenal."

West Ham's Martin Allen[15]

When the final whistles blow, the contrast in emotions at Anfield and Upton Park can't be more pronounced. In London's East End, it's frustration and misery for Manchester United…

"It was nine months of hard work and fighting, gone down the drain. … All in all it was the worst feeling I've ever had in football."

Manchester United defender Gary Pallister[16]

··

But Blackburn Rovers, thanks to the management of Kenny Dalglish, the glut of goals from Alan Shearer and the financial backing of owner Jack Walker, win the title – their first since the 1913/14 season…

"Sometimes you get a feeling about what is going to happen and on the last day I never felt we were going to lose it … I still thought we were going to win the league."

Kenny Dalglish recalls Blackburn's day in the sun at Anfield.[17]

"What we achieved that season will be remembered for a hell of long time in these parts, I'm sure. I'll never forget it … It was a magnificent season."

Blackburn striker and that season's Golden Boot winner, Alan Shearer.[18]

Games Played: 42

Pos	Team	GD	Pts
1	Blackburn Rovers	+41	89
2	Manchester United	+49	88
3	Nottingham Forest	+29	77
4	Liverpool	+28	74
5	Leeds United	+21	73
6	Newcastle United	+20	72
7	Tottenham Hotspur	+8	62
8	Queens Park Rangers	+2	60
9	Wimbledon	-17	56
10	Southampton	-2	54
11	Chelsea	-5	54
12	Arsenal	+3	51
13	Sheffield Wednesday	-8	51
14	West Ham United	-4	50
15	Everton	-7	50
16	Coventry City	-18	50
17	Manchester City	-11	49
18	Aston Villa	-5	48
19	Crystal Palace	-15	45
20	Norwich City	-17	43
21	Leicester City	-35	29
22	Ipswich Town	-57	27

CHAMPIONS: Blackburn Rovers

RUNNERS-UP: Manchester United

RELEGATED: Crystal Palace, Norwich City, Leicester City, Ipswich Town

PROMOTED: Middlesbrough, Bolton Wanderers

TOP GOALSCORER: Alan Shearer, Blackburn Rovers – 34

PLAYER OF THE SEASON: Alan Shearer, Blackburn Rovers

MANAGER OF THE SEASON: Kenny Dalglish, Liverpool

DID YOU KNOW? *Kenny Dalglish became only the third manager after Herbert Chapman (Huddersfield Town and Arsenal) and Brian Clough (Derby County and Nottingham Forest) to win league titles with two different clubs.*

PREMIER LEAGUE 1995/96

That's Entertainment

It's the year when the top flight was reduced to just 20 teams and it's also the first time that Manchester United have started a Premier League campaign not as the defending champions, having conceded their title to Blackburn Rovers.

It's all change at Old Trafford, too, where manager Alex Ferguson has moved on established stars like Paul Ince, Andrei Kanchelskis and Mark Hughes and promoted a host of youngsters, including Paul Scholes, Gary and Phil Neville, Nicky Butt, Ryan Giggs and David Beckham, to the first team.

As Bruce Rioch is appointed as the successor to George Graham at Arsenal, he makes an immediate impact, luring the classy Dutch striker Dennis Bergkamp to Highbury for £7.5 million.

"If Bergkamp thinks he's gonna set the world alight he can forget it. When the fog, ice and cold arrive, he won't want to know."

Alan Sugar, Tottenham chairman[1]

Meanwhile, on Tyneside, Newcastle United boss Kevin Keegan has assembled an attractive side that are being tipped for great things and this just three seasons after they so nearly dropped down to the old Third Division.

Bold, brave and seemingly obsessed with attacking, they have been nicknamed 'The Entertainers'.

And it's a tag they certainly live up to.

The season begins on 19 August and Aston Villa are hosting Manchester United at Villa Park…

"It's Dwight Yorke who's placed the ball on the spot, looking for Villa's third and we've played just over 35 minutes. And there are real worries for Alex Ferguson."

Tony Gubba, BBC *Match of the Day* commentator, as a rampant Aston Villa go three goals up before halftime.[2]

"The FA Carling Premiership ... Aston Villa 3 Manchester United 1."

James Alexander Gordon, BBC Radio 5 Live classified results[3]

"You can't win anything with kids."

BBC's *Match of the Day* analyst Alan Hansen openly criticises Alex Ferguson's decision to field six players under 20 in the defeat against Aston Villa.[4]

The early weeks of the season see a new cult hero emerge, in the shape of Leeds United's Anthony 'Tony' Yeboah, a Ghanaian striker with a gift for the spectacular...

"Yeboah with a chance ... what a stunning goal ... Tony Yeboah!"

Following a double against West Ham in Leeds' opener, Yeboah's outrageous winner at Liverpool leaves jaws on the floor across the country, as told by Sky Sports' Martin Tyler.[5]

"I hate that goal. I spent quite a few weeks afterwards moaning about the fact that I should have saved it. The commentator said about 30 seconds beforehand 'all this game needs is a goal' – and then Tony Yeboah turns up and scores."

And what it feels like to be beaten by Yeboah, courtesy of Liverpool keeper David James.[6]

"Yeboah ... On he goes. OHHHHH! Even by his standards that's breathtakingly brilliant ... It doesn't need any words, just wonderment really."

Sky Sports' commentator Martin Tyler fails to find the words to describe Tony Yeboah's mesmerising run and net-busting half-volley in Leeds' 4-2 victory at Wimbledon.[7]

"I used to say that it was the Yorkshire puddings that gave me the strength to score goals. It was just fun. My feet scored the goals. And my mind."

Tony Yeboah reveals the secret of his success.[8]

There's also a high-profile return for Eric Cantona, the Manchester United striker banned for eight months after attacking a spectator at Selhurst Park in January 1995. In typically charismatic fashion, he scores on his return against Liverpool and, soon after, scores an outrageous chip against Sunderland at Old Trafford...

"Here's Cantona ... He's done it! That is magnificent from Cantona! And after all his problems, his lack of form and the criticism that's come his way there is the perfect riposte!"

BBC commentator Jon Champion is there to witness one of the goals of the season.[9]

On 7 October, Middlesbrough announce the signing of Juninho, one of the world's most talented youngsters and the Brazilian Player of the Year. Boro fans welcome their new signing to the club by wearing sombreros, seemingly oblivious to the fact that he hails from Brazil and not Mexico.

"It is a measure of Middlesbrough's ambition that we have signed the most sought-after player in the world. We have beaten all the top Premiership clubs and several big European clubs to his signature. The negotiations between the two clubs were long and drawn out, but Juninho always wanted to come to Middlesbrough."

A proud Middlesbrough chief executive Keith Lamb on the club's transfer coup. The club will finish the season in 12th place.[10]

After nine games, Kevin Keegan's Newcastle United sit proudly on top of the Premier League with a four-point lead, having won eight of their nine games. Their tenth match is at home to Wimbledon, a game that sees them reach new heights, crushing the south Londoners 6-1 with Les Ferdinand scoring a hat trick.

> "I remember Kevin saying all the time: football is
> entertainment. Go out and entertain the crowd."
>
> Magpies' midfielder Rob Lee[11]

Newcastle continued their dominance throughout November 1995, winning games against Liverpool, Leeds and the champions Blackburn Rovers. By Christmas they are 10 points clear at the top of the table and looking untouchable. Their next match is at Old Trafford against their nearest challengers, Manchester United. They lose 2-0, a defeat made all the more galling by the fact that their former striker, Andy Cole, scored the opening goal.

The 10-point lead is down to seven but Newcastle win their next five to lead by 12 points by the end of January. No team in the history of the Premier League has been this far in front so late in the season and not gone on to win the title.

Typically, Kevin Keegan doesn't decide to bolster his defence with the Premier League title within reach. He goes out and buys another striker. And not just any striker, but the Colombian international Faustino 'Tino' Asprilla, a mercurial talent who is equal parts genius and screwball.

> *"He was different. You're going for the title and you've got all this
> pressure on and you've got someone who can fall over the ball
> one minute, then be the best player in the world and get you a
> goal the next."*
>
> Newcastle defender John Beresford[12]

In early March the Premier League's top two go head to head at Newcastle's St James' Park. In a one-sided game, the Magpies lay waste to the Manchester United goal. But they still lose 0-1, thanks to a goal from Eric Cantona and a heroic performance by United's goalkeeper Peter Schmeichel. Now, having been 12 points in front just four games ago, Newcastle's lead has been reduced to one.

"We'll carry on playing like this or I will go."

Newcastle United manager, Kevin Keegan[13]

"Tyneside is in turmoil. A glimpse at the letters page of the local papers will tell you as much. From Worried of Wallsend to Cynical of south Gosforth, the fear is that Newcastle have blown it. Not just with a pop and a splutter, either, but with a bloody great 12-point bang."

Ian Potts, *The Independent*[14]

With seven games to play, Newcastle United are three points behind Manchester United but they do have two games in hand on the league leaders. Kevin Keegan's team travel to Anfield to face his old club, Liverpool. It will go down in history as arguably the greatest game in the history of the Premier League. When the match begins, Liverpool are ahead within two minutes…

> **"And they've produced the perfect start! And who's got it? You can guess it! It's Robbie Fowler!"**
>
> Martin Tyler, Sky Sports commentator[15]

But Newcastle equalise on 10 minutes…

"Asprilla has been back to Colombia since he last played for Newcastle … And here he is, past Ruddock … Ferdinand turns … and scores!"

Martin Tyler, Sky Sports commentator[16]

"We'd named an attacking side but said beforehand that we didn't want to concede early and let the crowd get behind them. That worked out well… So we went on the attack."

More tactical astuteness from Les Ferdinand.[17]

> "Even after 10 minutes it felt like a game on the playground."
>
> Magpies' midfielder Rob Lee[18]

Four minutes later, the visitors have the lead…

> *"Ferdinand … That's great play! The control and the pass for Ginola … He's run beyond McAteer — 2-1 to Newcastle."*
>
> Martin Tyler, Sky Sports commentator[19]

The second half starts and Liverpool level matters in the 55th minute…

"McAteer … McManaman … We'll see how Newcastle can defend here … Fowler! Brilliant Liverpool goal by a brilliant young talent! Newcastle ripped apart!"

Martin Tyler, Sky Sports commentator[20]

But Liverpool are only level for two minutes…

> **"Terrific play from Beardsley, Newcastle respond the only way they know how with brilliant attacking play of their own … Asprilla! Rob Lee curled it through for him. Newcastle lead again."**
>
> Martin Tyler, Sky Sports commentator[21]

Yet again, Liverpool peg Newcastle back…

"McAteer … Oh that's a wicked ball … Collymore! Liverpool's quality is there again and Newcastle's prayers might not yet have been answered."

Martin Tyler, Sky Sports commentator[22]

Then, deep into injury time…

> **"Collymore closing in … LIVERPOOL LEAD IN STOPPAGE TIME!"**
>
> Sky Sports commentator Martin Tyler erupts as Liverpool steal a thrilling 4-3 win.[23]

"I didn't know what to feel after. It was fantastic. I ran over to the Kop and was thinking: 'What have I done?'"

Liverpool's match-winner Stan Collymore.[24]

"That was kamikaze football. Great for the fans but realistically nobody will win the championship defending every week like these teams did tonight."

Roy Evans, Liverpool manager[25]

"When I look back now, just seeing Kevin Keegan sprawled across the advertising hoardings, I think he was a beaten man after that."

Liverpool and England midfielder Jamie Redknapp[26]

"I remember saying: 'I should be despondent but I am not.' For me, then and now, the question is, 'What is success?' It isn't only about winning, but playing in a certain way."

Newcastle manager Kevin Keegan on the football philosophy that would be his undoing.[27]

In mid-April, Manchester United's fine form is curtailed by a 3-1 defeat at Southampton. The Red Devils are three goals down at halftime, prompting manager Alex Ferguson to change his side's 'invisible' grey shirts at the break.

They still lose 3-1.

"The players couldn't pick each other out. They said it was difficult to see their teammates at distance when they lifted their heads."

Manchester United manager Alex Ferguson[28]

"We wore blue and white in the second half, and played a bit better. I'd probably put it down to a mixture of the new kit and the manager's hairdryer treatment at halftime ..."

United midfielder Lee Sharpe[29]

Soon after, Manchester United defeat 10-man Leeds United at Old Trafford, despite a gutsy effort from their rivals. Indeed, Leeds' stubborn resistance is such that it leads Manchester United boss Alex Ferguson to argue that some teams and players always seem to try harder against his side, suggesting that Nottingham Forest, one of Newcastle's upcoming opponents, may give the Magpies an easy ride too.

It's a comment that enrages his Newcastle counterpart Kevin Keegan, who, after a 1-0 win over Leeds on 29 April, vents his anger live in the post-match television interview.

"When you do that with footballers like he said about Leeds, and when you do things like that about a man like Stuart Pearce … I've kept really quiet but I'll tell you something, he [Ferguson] went down in my estimation when he said that. We have not resorted to that. You can tell him now, we're still fighting for this title and he's got to go to Middlesbrough and get something. And I'll tell you, honestly, I will love it if we beat them. Love it."

Newcastle manager Kevin Keegan, live on Sky Sports, falls victim to Alex Ferguson's infamous 'mind games'. It's the beginning of the end for Newcastle's title challenge.[30]

> "It was extraordinary. That sort of thing just didn't happen. You couldn't help but get the sense that this was the end of Kevin Keegan."
>
> Sky Sports News reporter Nick Collins shares the shock he and his colleagues felt at Keegan's outburst.[31]

> *"Watching that game, we all came in the next day to training and we were all laughing about it. We were young but even as players, we knew we'd got to Kevin and Newcastle … we came into training and knew we'd won the league by then."*
>
> Midfielder David Beckham reveals just how Alex Ferguson's mind games went down with the Manchester United squad.[32]

The final day of the 1995/6 season. At the wrong end of the table, Southampton, Coventry City and Manchester City are all level on points going into the final day, with Bolton Wanderers and QPR already relegated.

Remarkably, City spend the last 10 minutes of their final game against Liverpool by taking the ball into the corner and wasting time, mistakenly believing that the 2-2 scoreline is good enough to keep them up.

It isn't.

"It looks like City are trying to run down the clock!"

BBC's baffled commentator Tony Gubba[33]

> **"Nobody told me there would be days like this and it's a bit hard to swallow."**
>
> Manchester City's striker Niall Quinn struggles to comprehend what happened.[34]

At the other end, meanwhile, Newcastle go into their final match needing to beat Spurs at home and hope – against hope – that Manchester United will lose at Middlesbrough if they're to win their first top-flight title since 1927.

It's not to be.

Newcastle can only manage a 1-1 draw against Tottenham while Manchester United breeze to a 3-0 win over Boro to take the title.

> *"People called the Newcastle team of 1996 with Kevin Keegan exciting – but they were exciting losers."*
>
> Gary Neville, Sky Sports pundit and former Manchester United full-back.[35]

"I really think they should have won the league in the 1995–96 season. If you're 12 points clear, out of all other competitions and have no major injury problems, you must have a fair chance."

Mark Lawrenson, employed as a defensive coach at Newcastle for the 1996/7 season.[36]

"People say we should have played more defensively once we got 12 points clear. I always say imagine playing that well to get 12 points clear then I go in the dressing room and play a couple more defenders and say I'm not going to play David Ginola or Rob Lee. Why would I want to do that?"

Newcastle manager Kevin Keegan, defiant in the face of defeat.[37]

But it's Manchester United's third Premier League title in four seasons and with 'Fergie's Fledglings' running the show, they go on to win the League and FA Cup double.

"That line pretty much made me, simply because I got it so dramatically wrong ... You can go a while without people mentioning it, but it is never far away."

Some final words from Alan Hansen on the words that continue to haunt him to this day.[38]

Games Played: 38

Pos	Team	GD	Pts
1	Manchester United	+38	82
2	Newcastle United	+29	78
3	Liverpool	+36	71
4	Aston Villa	+17	63
5	Arsenal	+17	63
6	Everton	+20	61
7	Blackburn Rovers	+14	61
8	Tottenham Hotspur	+12	61
9	Nottingham Forest	-4	58
10	West Ham United	-9	51
11	Chelsea	+2	50
12	Middlesbrough	-15	43
13	Leeds United	-17	43
14	Wimbledon	-15	41
15	Sheffield Wednesday	-13	40
16	Coventry City	-18	38
17	Southampton	-18	38
18	Manchester City	-25	38
19	Queens Park Rangers	-19	33
20	Bolton Wanderers	-32	29

CHAMPIONS: Manchester United

RUNNERS-UP: Newcastle United

RELEGATED: Manchester City, Queens Park Rangers, Bolton Wanderers

PROMOTED: Leicester City, Derby County, Sunderland

TOP GOALSCORER: Alan Shearer, Newcastle United – 31

PLAYER OF THE SEASON: Les Ferdinand, Newcastle United

MANAGER OF THE SEASON: Alex Ferguson, Manchester United

DID YOU KNOW? *Newcastle United spent 212 days at the top of the table in the season, the most in Premier League history for a side not to be crowned champions.*

PREMIER LEAGUE 1996/97

Farewell to The King

"Good evening," says Des Lynam, as he introduces the first Match of the Day of the new 1996/7 season. "It's only 47 days since Euro 96. I still think the Germans were lucky."

Yes, after the hopes of a nation were shattered in that semi-final heartache, the new Premiership season began with the domestic game in rude health. It's been a momentous few weeks in the transfer market too, especially at Newcastle United where manager Kevin Keegan assuages the fears of the club's fans in the wake of the sale of Andy Cole by smashing the world record transfer fee, paying £15 million for Blackburn's Alan Shearer, a local lad and lifelong Magpies' fan to boot.

"This signing is for the people of Newcastle. It just shows you the ambition of Newcastle United ... We're not the biggest, most successful team, but we're the biggest thinking club."

Newcastle manager Kevin Keegan[1]

For Shearer, it was the dream move he had always craved – and it had been a long time in the making, having had an unsuccessful trial at the club in 1982.

"I told them I was a centre-forward but they played me in goal for two days."

Newcastle and England striker Alan Shearer[2]

Chelsea sign Italy's Gianluca Vialli and make Ruud Gullit their player-manager, while Liverpool let their legendary striker Ian Rush head across the Pennines to Leeds United.

35

After just a single season in charge at Highbury, Bruce Rioch's time as Arsenal manager comes to a sudden end. Stewart Houston is placed in temporary charge as the Gunners seek a suitable replacement.

All the headlines of the opening day's action are dominated by one young man and one extraordinary goal. At Selhurst Park, Manchester United's 21-year-old midfielder David Beckham spots Wimbledon goalkeeper Neil Sullivan off his line and, from the halfway line, scores a goal that will launch his career into the football stratosphere.

> **"You have seen the goal of the season already ... I have never seen it done before. Pelé is the only one who came close to doing the same. Nayim? That was a miskick. But Beckham? It was marvellous. A truly tremendous strike."**
>
> United manager Alex Ferguson[3]

Well, not quite all of the headlines. At Middlesbrough, new recruit Fabrizio Ravanelli, a £7 million signing fresh from scoring the winner in the European Cup Final for Juventus against Ajax, plunders a sensational debut hat trick in a 3-3 draw against Liverpool and unveils his trademark shirt-over-the-head goal celebration.

> **"My favourite moment was undoubtedly my Premier League debut — the hattrick against Liverpool which was even voted as the best debut in Premier League history. That was my best moment, even if there were many."**
>
> Fabrizio Ravanelli, still talking the talk in 2016.[4]

It would prove to be a solid start to the season for Boro's star-studded new side. They beat West Ham 4-1, hammered Coventry 4-0, and when they won away at Everton they climbed to fourth place in the table. But when they lost at home to Arsenal, with goals by John Hartson and Ian Wright, it prompted a dismal run of form that saw them winless right up until Boxing Day.

On 14 September, Arsenal captain Tony Adams reveals that he is an alcoholic and will be taking a break from the game to seek help.

"It took a lot of bottle for Tony Adams to admit to being an alcoholic."

Ian Wright, Adams' Arsenal teammate[5]

....

It's the end of an era at Leeds United as they sack the man who led them out of the second tier of English football and on to the final First Division title, Howard 'Sgt. Wilko' Wilkinson. He is replaced by former Arsenal manager George Graham, who returns to management after serving a year's ban for receiving unsolicited payments.

> **"A manager must lay down at any club that he is the leader, more than the chairman, more than any star player ... I believe that 99% of people prefer to be led. Only 1% are leaders."**
>
> George Graham[6]

....

Despite being heavily linked with Barcelona coach Johan Cruyff, Arsenal finally find a new manager, appointing 46-year-old Frenchman Arsène Wenger, who arrives in North London after managerial spells at Nancy, Monaco and Japanese side Nagoya Grampus 8. But it's an appointment met with bewilderment by many Arsenal fans – and the players.

"It is a measure of the insularity of the English game that when Arsène Wenger's name emerged as Arsenal's favoured candidate for their vacant manager's job many supporters were asking: 'Arsène who?'"

Glenn Moore, *The Independent*[7]

> **"At first, I thought: What does this Frenchman know about football? He wears glasses and looks more like a schoolteacher. He's not going to be as good as George [Graham]. Does he even speak English properly?"**
>
> Arsenal skipper Tony Adams[8]

"I could understand the public not knowing who I was but I was surprised the specialists didn't. I'd taken Monaco to the Cup Winners' Cup final [in 1992], helped them to win the league [1988] and won the cup three times [1989, 1990, 1991]. But it didn't bother me much because at the end of the day that meant they had low expectations of me."

Arsène Wenger[9]

"I tried to watch the Tottenham match on television in my hotel yesterday, but I fell asleep."

Arsène Wenger, in his first press conference as Arsenal manager.[10]

Wenger gets straight to work on his squad and his chief concern is eradicating some of the bad habits the players have, especially the dietary ones.

"I changed a few habits of the players, which isn't easy in a team where the average age is 30 years."

Arsène Wenger[11]

Despite Tony Adams' absence, Arsenal's form shows no sign of faltering, with just one defeat in their first 12 games taking them to the top of the league, with the new French midfielder Patrick Vieira gaining rave reviews for his performances.

"He was in Holland, he was there to sign but I knew his agents. I spoke to Patrick and said, 'Please, stop. Come to Arsenal.' ... I just had the right luck to intervene at the right moment."

Arsène Wenger on how he convinced Vieira to join the Gunners – even though he wasn't yet the Arsenal manager.[12]

Following six consecutive wins, Newcastle United welcome Manchester United to St James' Park on 20 October and after losing out to Alex Ferguson's side in the title race in the previous season, the Magpies restore some pride with a memorable and, at times, mesmerising 5-0 victory.

"I always remember standing at the top of the steps as the Manchester United players left the ground. The last one out was Eric Cantona and he shook my hand and said, 'You've got a ***** good team'. His English was perfect. You've got to enjoy those moments."**

Magpies' manager Kevin Keegan[13]

The following week United shipped yet more goals, going down 6-3 at Southampton with Saints' new Norwegian striker, Egil Ostenstad, bagging a sensational hat trick.

"It turned out to be a surreal experience for me because I ended up scoring a hattrick … Four weeks earlier, I had been watching them on television back in Norway."

Egil Ostenstad[14]

While another United loss a week later, this time to Chelsea, had many commentators writing off their title chances, nothing could have been further from the truth as the Red Devils then embarked on a 16-match unbeaten run, largely inspired by the form of their talismanic Frenchman, Eric Cantona. In a 5-0 win over Sunderland, Cantona scored one of the goals of the season, deftly chipping the Black Cats' French goalkeeper Lionel Perez and then standing still, chest out, to accept the applause of the Old Trafford crowd.

"My grandma was there and after the game she said, 'Have you seen all these French flags? They are for you.' It was funny because she didn't realise they were not for me, but for Eric!"

Sunderland goalkeeper Lionel Perez[15]

In November, Southampton manager Graeme Souness announces the signing of Ali Dia. The Senegalese striker arrives at The Dell on the recommendation of his cousin and former FIFA World Player of the Year, George Weah. But all is not as it seems. Not only is Weah no relation to Dia but Souness has been duped into thinking he was by a friend of Dia's pretending to be the AC Milan great.

His one and only game for the Saints, when he comes on as a first-half substitute against Leeds, goes down in history for all the wrong reasons and he's substituted before the end of the game.

"His performance was almost comical ... He was just wandering everywhere ... It was all a bit embarrassing, and it became a taboo subject with the manager.

Dia's Southampton teammate Matt Le Tissier[16]

Claiming unprecedented illness in their squad, Middlesbrough fail to fulfil their away fixture at Blackburn Rovers in December. They are later docked three points for their actions by the Football Association, points that would ultimately prove vital come the end of the season.

"I reckon we will be relegated, I'm almost certain of it."

Boro striker Fabrizio Ravanelli[17]

"One of the players had gone home and he phoned me up and said he'd seen on Sky Sports that Middlesbrough weren't going to turn up because they had 'flu. He said 'Have you seen this? They're not coming.' It was just unbelievable. I'd never heard of anything like that happening in football."

Blackburn manager Tony Parkes isn't too impressed by Middlesbrough's no-show.[18]

Shock waves reverberate around Newcastle in early January as manager Kevin Keegan surprisingly calls time on his tenure at St James' Park with his team in fourth place in the league. He is replaced by former Liverpool and Blackburn Rovers manager Kenny Dalglish.

"It was my decision alone. I feel I have taken the club as far as I can and that it would be in the best interest of all concerned if I resign now."

Kevin Keegan's statement[19]

"They called it Black Wednesday on Tyneside. People cried in the streets or stared at each other in stunned silence."

The *Newcastle Chronicle* newspaper laments Keegan's departure.[20]

"People are saying that Kevin leaving is like the Queen dying, but it's worse than that."

John Regan, secretary of Newcastle Independent Supporters' Association[21]

There's another seven-goal thriller at Anfield in March as Liverpool and Newcastle stage a repeat of the remarkable 4-3 result from the previous season. Three goals down at halftime, Newcastle stage a thrilling comeback, only to be undone by Robbie Fowler's injury-time headed winner.

> **"They've done it! Incredible! Fowler! It's a repeat 12 months on and Liverpool are back in front!"**
>
> Alan Parry, Sky Sports commentator[22]

Despite a star-studded squad packed with international talent like Fabrizio Ravanelli, the Brazilian Emerson and his compatriot and the Player of the Year, Juninho, and having reached both the final of the FA Cup (where they lost to Chelsea) and the League Cup (where they were beaten in a replay by Leicester City), Middlesbrough had still managed to be relegated. They are joined by Sunderland and rock-bottom Nottingham Forest.

> **"The subsequent three-point deduction was the difference between safety and relegation. It was a shambolic end after a scintillating start and proved that the foundations were weak. They were simply never built to last."**
>
> Omar Saleem, *Guardian* journalist[23]

Manchester United, meanwhile, seal the title with two games to spare as closest challengers Newcastle fail to win away at West Ham. It had hardly been a vintage campaign for the Red Devils but they had topped the table from the start of February and never looked back.

United's celebrations would be tempered, however, by a bolt from the blue as their star player, Eric Cantona, announces his retirement from the game, aged just 30. With five championship titles in five years in England, he leaves the game at the very top.

> **"Football lost its excitement for me. That's why I retired. I didn't have to retire, I was still fit, I was still good ... But I got a bit bored."**
>
> Eric Cantona[24]

"If ever there was one player, anywhere in the world, that was made for Manchester United, it was Cantona. He swaggered in, stuck his chest out, raised his head and surveyed everything as though he were asking: 'I'm Cantona. How big are you? Are you big enough for me?'"

Manchester United manager Alex Ferguson[25]

Games Played: 38

Pos	Team	GD	Pts
1	Manchester United	+32	75
2	Newcastle United	+33	68
3	Arsenal	+30	68
4	Liverpool	+25	68
5	Aston Villa	+13	61
6	Chelsea	+3	59
7	Sheffield Wednesday	-1	57
8	Wimbledon	+3	56
9	Leicester City	-8	47
10	Tottenham Hotspur	-7	46
11	Leeds United	-10	46
12	Derby County	-13	46
13	Blackburn Rovers	-1	42
14	West Ham United	-9	42
15	Everton	-13	42
16	Southampton	-6	41
17	Coventry City	-16	41
18	Sunderland	-18	40
19	Middlesbrough	-9	39*
20	Nottingham Forest	-28	34

* Middlesbrough docked three points

CHAMPIONS: Manchester United

RUNNERS-UP: Newcastle United

RELEGATED: Sunderland, Middlesbrough, Nottingham Forest

PROMOTED: Bolton Wanderers, Barnsley, Crystal Palace

TOP GOALSCORER: Alan Shearer, Newcastle United – 25

PLAYER OF THE SEASON: Alan Shearer, Newcastle United

MANAGER OF THE SEASON: Alex Ferguson, Manchester United

DID YOU KNOW? *Manchester United won their fourth Premier League title with just 75 points, winning the division with the lowest total ever achieved.*

The Wenger Revolution

As the Premier League entered its sixth season, it had yet to be won by a team outside Lancashire. Having spent 26 long years chasing the top flight, Manchester United had found the new competition much more to their liking and had embarked on a period of dominance not seen since the Liverpool side of the 1980s.

But the south was about to rise again…

It's Arsène Wenger's first full season in charge at Arsenal and he's spent the summer assembling a side and a squad that seems set to challenge for honours. He brings in Emmanuel Petit, Christopher Wreh and Gilles Grimandi from Monaco and one of the quickest wingers in the game, Ajax's Marc Overmars.

It's a different story in south London, where Wimbledon manager Joe Kinnear is struggling to keep up with the rest of the division.

> **"It's like going into a nuclear war with bows and arrows."**
>
> Wimbledon manager Joe Kinnear's cash-strapped club struggles to compete in the Premiership.[1]

The sudden departure of Eric Cantona from Manchester United, meanwhile, sees Alex Ferguson sign a replacement in the shape of the former Spurs and England striker Teddy Sheringham in a £3.5 million deal.

> **"I remember Alex Ferguson telling me when I first signed: 'You won't believe what it's like to play for Man. United.' And I was like, 'Yeah, yeah, yeah.' But he was right."**
>
> Teddy Sheringham recalls his move to Old Trafford.[2]

In his first league game for United, Sheringham returns to White Hart Lane and is greeted, predictably, with a hostile reaction. In the 60th minute, United are awarded a penalty and Sheringham takes it. To the delight of the home crowd, he hits the post. But United have the last laugh, with two late goals giving them the points.

> **"Those goals were a bit of a relief. I felt confident taking the penalty and I'll take another."**
>
> Teddy Sheringham[3]

While United's new striker takes time to settle, Arsenal's star forward Dennis Bergkamp seems to be playing a different game to everyone else. In a breathtaking display against Leicester City at Filbert Street, the former Ajax striker scores a hat trick that has gone down in history as one of the best the division has witnessed.

The first goal is a 20-yard right-foot screamer that steams into the top corner, while the second is a breakaway goal with a clever dinked finish over Foxes' keeper Kasey Keller at the end.

But the third is the best of the lot.

As David Platt loops a through ball into the Leicester box, Bergkamp pulls it out of the night sky with his right foot, juggles back over his shoulder with his left, leaving defender Matt Elliott on his backside, and then slots it past Keller into the far corner.

That month, Bergkamp would go on to take the top three places in *Match of the Day's* Goal of the Month competition, the one and only time a player has swept the board in the competition.

Nobody ever mentions that Arsenal only drew 3-3 that night though.

> **"That game was all about Bergkamp. He was on fire and it was one of the finest individual displays I ever came up against."**
>
> Steve Walsh, Leicester captain. The Foxes' defender scored a late equaliser in that game.[4]

> **"Whenever Dennis gets the ball now I feel that something positive is going to happen."**
>
> Arsène Wenger, Arsenal manager[5]

But Arsenal's 12-game unbeaten start to the season comes to a shuddering halt at the beginning of November when they lose 3-0 at Derby County. Though they defeat Manchester United 3-2 in their next game, they lose three of their next four games, dropping from first to fifth in the table.

It's a slump that allows United to move into their now customary position at the top of the table. At times, the Red Devils are in imperious form. They blow away Barnsley 7-0 and Sheffield Wednesday 6-1 in successive games and beat Wimbledon 5-2, Blackburn 4-0 and Liverpool 3-1 in the games after the Arsenal defeat.

Across north London, meanwhile, there's a new man in place at White Hart Lane as Gerry Francis resigns as Tottenham boss. He is replaced by the Swiss Christian Gross, who arrives late from Heathrow Airport for his first press conference, brandishing a London Underground travel card.

> "I want this to become the ticket to the dreams."
>
> Christian Gross, new Spurs manager[6]

"I'm sure it will be a case of 'Christian Who?' for a lot of people, but they were saying 'Arsène Who?' when Wenger took over at Arsenal."

Clive Wilson, Tottenham's defender[7]

The new year sees Spurs in the relegation zone and it takes the return of their cult hero Jurgen Klinsmann to help them out of the mire. In his second spell at the club, the German international scores nine goals in 15 matches, four of which come in a 6-2 hammering of Wimbledon, helping the team to pull away from the wrong end of the table.

> **"Christian called me up and asked if there was any chance of me coming in to start against Arsenal."**
>
> Jurgen Klinsmann explains how his return to White Hart Lane came about.[8]

It's February and Ruud Gullit is a surprise casualty at Chelsea as he fails to agree a new contract at Stamford Bridge. It comes as a shock to the Blues' player-manager, however, who believed that negotiations were still ongoing. He is replaced by fans' favourite Gianluca Vialli.

"I was astounded to find out from the media that I have been replaced as Chelsea coach by Gianluca Vialli ... I am committed to Chelsea, and in particular to the fans, whose dreams I have tried so hard to fulfil."

Ruud Gullit[9]

> **"I have to say that I was amazed when Colin [Hutchinson, Chelsea Managing Director] asked me if I was available ... I'm still a little confused but I'm very happy."**
>
> Gianluca Vialli, new Chelsea manager[10]

As the season heads into March, it's Manchester United that seem destined to retain their Premiership title. Alex Ferguson's side now sit 12 points clear at the summit, although they have played three games more than nearest challengers Arsenal. It's a lead so healthy that one bookmaker even pays out on United being the league champions, despite there being 10 games to play.

But when the two sides meet at Old Trafford on 14 March, it's a game that changes the season's narrative.

It takes a late goal from Arsenal's Marc Overmars to decide the match and it's a victory that now leaves the Gunners just six points behind and still with three games in hand.

"I think United have still got a small advantage, because we have to take the points from the games in hand. But we have closed the gap, and it makes it very interesting for everybody until the end."

Arsène Wenger, Arsenal boss[11]

"If they win their games in hand they will go ahead of us, but they will find out they start dropping points towards the end of the season, there's no question about that."

Alex Ferguson, Manchester United manager[12]

What Ferguson didn't know was that virtually the only points Arsenal would drop would be in the game after they had won the title. The Gunners go on an astonishing nine-match winning streak, and with three games to play they host Everton at Highbury, needing a victory to wrap up the title.

And they do it in style.

With virtually the last kick of the game, Steve Bould's long ball finds his central defensive partner Tony Adams still upfield and as the Everton keeper Thomas Myhre comes out, the Arsenal skipper simply hammers the ball past him and into the net to complete a 4-0 rout.

> **"And it's Tony Adams put through by Steve Bould … would you believe it? That sums it all up."**
>
> Martin Tyler, Sky Sports commentator[13]

It's a fitting way for Arsenal – and Arsène Wenger – to win their first Premiership title and while the Gunners lose their final two games, allowing Manchester United to close the gap to just one point, there's no denying Arsenal's right to the top-flight title, not least because they won 45 points from a possible 51 between Boxing Day 1997 and 3 May 1998.

Six days after picking up the Premiership trophy, Arsenal took on Newcastle United in the FA Cup final at Wembley and with goals from Marc Overmars and Nicolas Anelka the Gunners cruised to the double, only the sixth time it has been achieved.

> **"It's just unbelievable. To come to England and win the double – I couldn't dream of it at the beginning of the season."**
>
> Arsène Wenger, Arsenal manager[14]

> **"This surpasses everything we have done in the past."**
>
> Lee Dixon, Arsenal defender[15]

There were many in the game – Arsenal captain Tony Adams included – who doubted Arsène Wenger's suitability when he arrived at Highbury in September 1996.

Nobody doubted him now.

Games Played: 38

Pos	Team	GD	Pts
1	Arsenal	+35	78
2	Manchester United	+47	77
3	Liverpool	+26	65
4	Chelsea	+28	63
5	Leeds United	+11	59
6	Blackburn Rovers	+5	58
7	Aston Villa	+1	57
8	West Ham United	-1	56
9	Derby County	+3	55
10	Leicester City	+10	53
11	Coventry City	+2	52
12	Southampton	-5	48
13	Newcastle United	-9	44
14	Tottenham Hotspur	-12	44
15	Wimbledon	-12	44
16	Sheffield Wednesday	-15	44
17	Everton	-15	40
18	Bolton Wanderers	-20	40
19	Barnsley	-45	35
20	Crystal Palace	-34	33

CHAMPIONS: Arsenal

RUNNERS-UP: Manchester United

RELEGATED: Crystal Palace, Bolton Wanderers, Barnsley

PROMOTED: Middlesbrough, Charlton Athletic, Nottingham Forest

TOP GOALSCORERS: Dion Dublin (Coventry City), Michael Owen (Liverpool), Chris Sutton (Blackburn Rovers) – 18

PLAYER OF THE SEASON: Dennis Bergkamp, Arsenal

MANAGER OF THE SEASON: Arsène Wenger, Arsenal

DID YOU KNOW? *All three sides that were promoted to the Premiership – Bolton, Barnsley and Crystal Palace – were relegated back to Division One in the 1997/8 season.*

Mind Games Over Matter

With the World Cup Finals in France over, the ever-increasing influx of foreign players arriving in the Premiership showed no sign of waning. Across the league, clubs were tempted by talent that, for the most part, was more readily available and cheaper than comparative British players. Whether it represented better value, however, was another matter entirely.

Arsenal, for example, land the Inter Milan star Nwankwo Kanu and Argentina's Nelson Vivas, while Manchester United land Dutch centre half Jaap Stam, Aston Villa's Dwight Yorke and winger Jesper Blomqvist in a £28 million spending spree.

Unusually, Liverpool also appoint former French national coach Gerard Houllier as a co-manager at Anfield to work alongside Roy Evans, while their neighbours across Stanley Park, Everton, turn to Rangers' coach Walter Smith to fill the void left by Howard Kendall's departure.

The season begins and after a summer where he had announced himself to the watching world with a sensational goal for England against Argentina, Liverpool's teenage sensation Michael Owen carries on where he left off, bludgeoning a brilliant hat trick at Newcastle in Ruud Gullit's first game in charge at the Magpies.

"What an unbelievable goal from Michael Owen! A hattrick inside 30-odd minutes! I've been watching Liverpool for over 40 years now and I thought Kenny Dalglish was the best Liverpool player I'd ever seen..."

Alan Parry, Sky Sports commentator, sings Owen's praises.[1]

"It was very interesting."

Ruud Gullit, new Newcastle manager[2]

As Sheffield Wednesday host Arsenal at Hillsborough, an ongoing spat between Paolo Di Canio and the Gunners' Patrick Vieira escalates into an ugly brawl and referee Paul Alcock decides to give the Owls' Italian midfielder his marching orders. But as Alcock brandishes the red card, Di Canio shoves the official in the chest, sending him hurtling to the turf.

> **"One moment can erase everything else you've accomplished in your career. I didn't kill anybody. I pushed a referee. We all know that's wrong. But it can happen ... Even now, when I watch it, I can't believe the way he [Alcock] went down ..."**
>
> Paolo Di Canio, who received an 11-match ban and a £10,000 fine.[3]

It proves to be a short-lived stay at Tottenham Hotspur for their Swiss coach Christian Gross. Just 10 months after his appointment, and having led Spurs to their worst league finish since 1994, he is sacked by chairman Alan Sugar just six weeks into the new season.

> **"He [Gross] would say things like, 'Today is Tottenham weather, we must not wave the white flag today, we must be strong.' ... We thought, 'Well that's all great, but how are you setting the team up?'"**
>
> John Scales, Spurs defender[4]

In a shock move, Gross is replaced by the former Arsenal manager George Graham, who leaves his job at Leeds United and returns to the capital. Predictably, his Arsenal association provokes unrest among Tottenham Hotspur supporters.

> **"I don't like it, but I can take it."**
>
> George Graham, new Spurs boss[5]

George Graham's departure from Leeds would see his assistant, David O'Leary, step into his first managerial role, after a long and ultimately fruitless pursuit of the Leicester City manager, Martin O'Neill.

> ## "He's done an outstanding job since he came to the club. We have to decide whether he can bridge the gap from being a No 2."
>
> Peter Ridsdale, Leeds United chairman. Despite doubts about his experience, the Irishman duly delivers, helping Leeds to a fourth-place finish and a spot in the following season's UEFA Cup.[6]

The Liverpool experiment fails. In mid-November, Roy Evans resigns as co-manager of the club, leaving Gerard Houllier to take the job on his own.

> ## "If it's not working then it would be a bigger mistake to stay. I want to give Gerard (Houillier) and the team a chance and to do that you have to walk away."
>
> Roy Evans[7]

Though they lose the opening game of the season to Coventry City, under their Italian manager, Gianluca Vialli, Chelsea embark on an unbeaten streak that lasts into the new year and sees them top the table at Christmas, thanks to the irrepressible form of Gianfranco Zola and new recruits like France's World Cup-winning defender Marcel Desailly, Spain's Albert Ferrer and Italian striker Pierluigi Casiraghi.

Chelsea's progress under Vialli sees them lose just three games all season but, as ever, it's Manchester United that force the issue, with their forwards in prolific form. In February, the Red Devils win five games in a row, including an 8-1 win at Nottingham Forest. It's a game also notable for substitute Ole Gunnar Solskjaer scoring four times in just 18 minutes, the most ever scored by a substitute in the competition.

In March, Wimbledon appoint coaches Mick Harford and Terry Burton to run first-team affairs as manager Joe Kinnear steps down because of health problems. The Dons' boss suffered a heart attack prior to the game against Sheffield Wednesday. He doesn't return to the club.

As United, Arsenal and Chelsea all vie for the title, George Graham's arrival at Tottenham steadies the ship. The Lilywhites finish in 11th place and win a berth in the UEFA Cup as they win the League Cup, beating Leicester City 1-0.

Four years after they were crowned the Premier League champions, meanwhile, Blackburn Rovers are relegated after a goalless draw against the leaders Manchester United at Ewood Park. It's an ignominious fall from grace for a club that had come so far under the ownership of Jack Walker.

"I don't think pound notes are going to do it, we need a spirit and heartbeat in this club. You need to develop it, build it up. If I get a base and foundation, I think I will do well."

Brian Kidd, Blackburn manager, on Rovers' plan to get back to the promised land of the Premier League. The former Manchester United assistant had replaced Roy Hodgson in November 1998.[8]

"It is sad for the club, you can see Jack Walker's eyes were all watery."

Kenny Dalglish, former Blackburn manager, who was at Ewood Park to see his old club relegated.[9]

Blackburn are joined in the drop by Nottingham Forest, who have been bottom since Christmas, and Charlton, relegated after Southampton, who have been in the bottom three since the second week of the season, beat Everton on the final day to pull clear of trouble.

In their penultimate game, Arsenal's title hopes suffer a hammer blow when they lose 1-0 away at Leeds United in a game they really should have won.

"It was a strange game ... It's unbelievable, we created so many chances and didn't score."

Arsène Wenger, Arsenal manager[10]

The defeat hands the initiative back to Manchester United, whose unbeaten run now stretches back to 19 December. They go into the final game needing a win against Spurs at Old Trafford to be assured of their fifth title in seven seasons.

As Arsenal do all they can do, beating Aston Villa 1-0 at Highbury, it's United that seal the deal, coming from a goal down to win 2-1.

The following week, United complete their third double, beating Newcastle in the final of the FA Cup at Wembley, leaving them just days away from completing an unprecedented treble in the Champions League Final against Bayern Munich. A goal down as the game goes into injury time, United equalise through Teddy Sheringham and, remarkably, snatch a last-gasp winner through substitute Ole Gunnar Solskjaer.

It's a mind-boggling end to a quite brilliant season for United and even Alex Ferguson is lost for words…

"Football, bloody hell."

Alex Ferguson, Manchester United manager[11]

Games Played: 38

Pos	Team	GD	Pts
1	Manchester United	+43	79
2	Arsenal	+42	78
3	Chelsea	+27	75
4	Leeds United	+28	67
5	West Ham United	-7	57
6	Aston Villa	+5	55
7	Liverpool	+19	54
8	Derby County	-5	52
9	Middlesbrough	-6	51
10	Leicester City	-6	49
11	Tottenham Hotspur	-3	47
12	Sheffield Wednesday	-1	46
13	Newcastle United	-6	46
14	Everton	-5	43
15	Coventry City	-12	42
16	Wimbledon	-23	42
17	Southampton	-27	41
18	Charlton Athletic	-15	36
19	Blackburn Rovers	-14	35
20	Nottingham Forest	-34	30

CHAMPIONS: Manchester United

RUNNERS-UP: Arsenal

RELEGATED: Charlton Athletic, Blackburn Rovers, Nottingham Forest

PROMOTED: Sunderland, Bradford City, Watford

TOP GOALSCORERS: Jimmy Floyd Hasselbaink (Leeds United), Michael Owen (Liverpool) and Dwight Yorke (Manchester United) – 18

PLAYER OF THE SEASON: David Ginola, Tottenham Hotspur

MANAGER OF THE SEASON: Alex Ferguson, Manchester United

DID YOU KNOW? *Manchester United's 8-1 win at Nottingham Forest is the highest away win in the history of the Premier League.*

Taking the Honours

The 1998/9 season had barely ended when, a little over a month since Manchester United won an unprecedented League, FA Cup and Champions League treble, the club's manager, Alex Ferguson, became 'Sir Alex Ferguson' as he received a knighthood in the Queen's Birthday Honours List.

> **"I see this as an honour not just for me, but for the people who have supported me through my life and made me what I am. If my parents were still alive, they would be very proud. They gave me a good start in life, the values that have driven me, and the confidence to believe in myself."**
>
> 'Sir' Alex Ferguson, football's latest knight.[1]

Yet United would not have the opportunity to defend their FA Cup. Under pressure from the Football Association, they withdrew from the competition to play in the FIFA World Club Championship instead, the FA believing that the club's participation in the event would boost their chances of winning the bid to host the 2006 World Cup Finals. It didn't.

> **"We had to think of the situation regarding England hosting the World Cup. No one wants to see them not get it. I dare not think of the criticism we would have received if we had refused. That was unthinkable – and that's a Scotsman talking."**
>
> Sir Alex Ferguson[2]

At Stamford Bridge, meanwhile, the increasingly cosmopolitan nature of the Chelsea squad under manager Gianluca Vialli was starting to present a few problems.

"Obviously there's a language barrier. The majority of the lads speak Italian, but there's a few who don't."

Dennis Wise, Chelsea skipper[3]

Just two days after securing the services of the Croatian star Davor Suker from Real Madrid, Arsenal signed France's 22-year-old Juventus striker Thierry Henry in a deal reported to be worth £11 million.

One of these two players would go on to become a club legend.

"Thierry Henry is a valuable addition to our squad. He is a young international striker who will be a great asset to Arsenal Football Club."

A valuable addition to the squad? Understatement of the century from Arsenal manager Arsène Wenger.[4]

"If you look at the whole package, with everything Henry has, I don't think you can find that anywhere else. You give him the ball in the right place and his acceleration will take him past any defender in the world."

Dennis Bergkamp, Henry's Arsenal teammate[5]

The season begins and the reigning champions Manchester United hit the ground running, winning six of their first seven matches to lead the league. They are only knocked off the top when their new goalkeeper, the Italian Massimo Taibi, allows the softest of shots from Southampton's Matt Le Tissier to squirm through his legs and into the net, gifting the Saints a point in a 3-3 draw at Old Trafford on 25 September.

"To this day, I do not know how it was even possible. The media were bad but it was part of our job – my team-mates were all wonderful with me. I used to think about it a lot but I don't as much anymore."

Massimo Taibi reflects on that fateful day at Old Trafford.[6]

The following week, United's run of 29 games without a defeat came to a crushing end at Stamford Bridge as they were thrashed 5-0 by Chelsea in an ill-tempered encounter that saw United's Nicky Butt sent off for kicking out at Dennis Wise. Not that the Chelsea man was entirely innocent.

> *"Dennis Wise was confirming his reputation as the most spiteful player in English football by scything down Nicky Butt then, word has it, tweaking the pubic hair of the Manchester United player."*
>
> Ian Ridley, *The Guardian*[7]

With four defeats in their opening five league games, Ruud Gullit tenders his resignation at Newcastle after a year in charge. The writing has been on the wall for the Dutchman since the day he drops fans' favourite Alan Shearer for the derby match against Sunderland at the end of August, a game they lose 2-1 at St James' Park.

To the fans' delight, he was replaced by the former England manager – and lifelong Newcastle fan – Bobby Robson.

The new coach makes an immediate impact as Newcastle hammer Sheffield Wednesday 8-0 in his first game in charge on 19 September, chalking up their first league win since April and their first home win since February. Man of the match is striker Alan Shearer, who plunders five goals before promptly popping the balloon of positivity around St James' Park.

"We must not get carried away. I'm sorry to bring everybody down to earth."

Alan Shearer[8]

There's a Premier League classic at Stamford Bridge in October as Arsenal come from two goals down against Chelsea and, thanks to a hat trick in the final 15 minutes by Nwanko Kanu, run out 3-2 winners. The Nigerian's third goal is a beauty as he chases the ball down and from the byline near the corner flag somehow manages to bend it into the top corner.

> "Whenever everybody sees me and it is something to do with Chelsea, even the fans in Nigeria, they are always trying to curse me and say, 'Why did you score that goal?' But then the Arsenal fans are happy."
>
> Nwanko Kanu, Arsenal's match-winner[9]

Come Christmas and it was David O'Leary's exciting young Leeds United side that were leading the pack, a run of 12 wins from 14 matches putting them clear of Manchester United and Arsenal.

"Ideally, I would like David O'Leary to be at this club for life."

Leeds United chairman Peter Ridsdale[10]

History was made on Boxing Day when, after 111 years, 3 months and 17 days of league football, Chelsea fielded the first entirely overseas line-up in English football for their game against Southampton. There was a Dutch goalkeeper, a defence from Spain, Brazil, France and Nigeria, a midfield consisting of a Swiss-born Italian, a Romanian, a Uruguayan and another Frenchman, and a strike force from Italy and Norway.

"We were used to playing with players of different nationalities, but we all spoke English in and around the training ground, so to us the nationalities meant nothing at all. Tore Andre Flo probably had the best English of anyone in the squad and he was Norwegian!"

Roberto Di Matteo, Chelsea midfielder[11]

In a thrilling encounter at the Boleyn Ground in February, West Ham edged out Bradford 5-4, thanks largely to a hat trick from Frank Lampard. But the game would be remembered not just for the scoreline but for the antics of the Hammers' Paolo Di Canio, who, having had three reasonable penalty appeals turned down by referee Neale Barry, demanded to be substituted by his manager, Harry Redknapp.

"I've no idea what he was saying. It was in Italian. But he understands English. I said, 'I don't care what you say in Italian, but if you wave your arms around once more I'll give you a yellow card."

Neale Barry, referee[12]

A month later, however, Paolo Di Canio showed exactly why Harry Redknapp was right to keep faith with the Italian, despite his emotional outbursts, when he scored a jaw-dropping volley against Wimbledon. It was a strike that would win the Goal of the Season award.

"Sinclair's cross ... over Cunningham's head ... DI CANIO! OH I DO NOT BELIEVE THAT! THAT IS SENSATIONAL ... EVEN BY HIS STANDARDS!"

Martin Tyler, Sky Sports commentator[13]

> **"Paolo did things with the ball that made you gasp. Other footballers would pay to watch him train."**
>
> Harry Redknapp, West Ham manager[14]

By April, Manchester United's progress towards another title seemed inexorable. They tore West Ham apart at Old Trafford, winning 7-1. They won away at Bradford 4-0 and beat Sunderland by the same score. When they beat Chelsea 3-2 at Old Trafford, it seemed like nobody could stop Alex Ferguson's free-scoring side.

When they beat Southampton 3-1 at The Dell, the title was theirs again, and all with four matches to spare.

"When we had the defeat against Newcastle I think we wakened up. We are now going to aim to win all our remaining games – I think this is the best Man Utd team we have ever had."

Sir Alex Ferguson, Manchester United manager[15]

And win their remaining games they did. United would end the season on an 11-game winning streak and leave the rest of the division trailing in their wake. Their margin of victory over second-placed Arsenal was 18 points – the biggest ever in the history of the Premier League. They had also scored a Premier League high of 97 goals to secure their sixth title in just eight years.

The third and final Champions League place would go to Leeds United who, despite some difficult results (including a run of four defeats in succession), managed to edge out Liverpool.

> **"The last six weeks we've been like a ship that has got three quarters of the way across the ocean and then the engine has gone, but we managed to limp into port."**
>
> David O'Leary, Leeds manager[16]

It's a tighter affair at the wrong end of the table, where Bradford City needed a header goal from David Wetherall on the final day of the season to give them the narrowest of wins over Liverpool. That victory saw the Bantams stay up on just 36 points – the lowest total ever to remain in the top flight. It also meant that Wimbledon, who lost 10 of their last 11 games, joined Sheffield Wednesday and Watford in the drop down a division – the first time they had been relegated from the Premier League. It also happened to be 12 years to the day since their famous FA Cup final win over Liverpool.

"Halle takes it ... OH WETHERALL'S FREE! FANTASTIC HEADER! BRADFORD CITY LEAD LIVERPOOL BY ONE GOAL TO NIL!"

Martin Tyler, Sky Sports commentator[17]

> **"That's something I will remember for the rest of my life. They have been writing us off all season and it gives us such satisfaction to prove them wrong."**
>
> David Wetherall, Bradford's saviour[18]

Games Played: 38

Pos	Team	GD	Pts
1	Manchester United	+52	91
2	Arsenal	+30	73
3	Leeds United	+15	69
4	Liverpool	+21	67
5	Chelsea	+19	65
6	Aston Villa	+11	58
7	Sunderland	+1	58
8	Leicester City	0	55
9	West Ham United	-1	55
10	Tottenham Hotspur	+8	53
11	Newcastle United	+9	52
12	Middlesbrough	-6	52
13	Everton	+10	50
14	Coventry City	-7	44
15	Southampton	-17	44
16	Derby County	-13	38
17	Bradford City	-30	36
18	Wimbledon	-28	33
19	Sheffield Wednesday	-32	31
20	Watford	-42	24

CHAMPIONS: Manchester United

RUNNERS-UP: Arsenal

RELEGATED: Wimbledon, Sheffield Wednesday, Watford

PROMOTED: Ipswich Town, Charlton Athletic, Manchester City

TOP GOALSCORER: Kevin Phillips, Sunderland – 30

PLAYER OF THE SEASON: Roy Keane, Manchester United

MANAGER OF THE SEASON: Alex Ferguson, Manchester United

DID YOU KNOW? *Manchester United didn't lose a single game at Old Trafford in the 1999/2000 season, while Coventry didn't win away in the entire campaign.*

Moneyball

For all their money, status and stellar playing rosters, Chelsea, Arsenal and Liverpool were still trailing in the wake of an all-conquering Manchester United side that showed no sign of giving up their Premiership title dominance without an almighty fight.

Certainly, the pretenders to their throne were intent on bolstering their ranks. Chelsea brought Jimmy Floyd Hasselbaink back to England after a season in Spain, and added the Croatian Mario Stanic. Arsenal waved farewell to Marc Overmars and Emmanuel Petit, both sold to Barcelona, and brought in Robert Pires, Sylvain Wiltord and Edu. Liverpool, meanwhile, lured Nicky Barmby across Stanley Park from Everton and made an inspired free transfer in bringing Gary McAllister in from Coventry.

As for Manchester United? All they did was add a new keeper to their ranks, the French World Cup winner Fabien Barthez.

Before the season starts, Martin O'Neill leaves as Leicester City manager, choosing not to renew his contract, and takes up the position of Celtic manager.

"I put my heart and soul into the club. It was as if Leicester City Football club was my club, my baby."

Martin O'Neill[1]

He is replaced by Peter Taylor, who hits the ground running at Filbert Street, guiding the Foxes to the top of table by the beginning of October, a position the club hadn't reached since 1963.

> "Everyone was very nervous when I took over as I was taking over from Martin O'Neill, who was such a legend at Leicester. The players weren't surprised about being top of the table, they just went onto the pitch believing they could win every match."
>
> Peter Taylor, new Leicester City manager[2]

Leicester's unbeaten eight-game start is so impressive that when Kevin Keegan walks out on England in October, it's Peter Taylor that's called upon to fill in as the temporary national manager.

Manchester United's seven-game unbeaten start would come to a spectacular end on 1 October when they lost 1-0 to Arsenal, thanks to one of the greatest goals in Premier League history. With half an hour gone, the Gunners' French striker Thierry Henry flicked the ball up on the edge of the United area with his back to goal, swivelled, and unleashed an unstoppable volley into the top corner, leaving the United keeper – and his French international teammate Fabien Barthez – utterly bewildered.

"When you haven't been scoring goals, sometimes you need to try something a little bit crazy something you don't have to think about but just do it."

Arsène Wenger, Arsenal manager[3]

"You can't do anything about a goal like that. I couldn't believe it."

Sir Alex Ferguson is forced to concede the brilliance of Henry's strike.[4]

There's also a new manager, or rather 'head coach', at Stamford Bridge, where the Italian Claudio Ranieri steps into the hot seat vacated by his compatriot Gianluca Vialli, sacked after just one win in his first four games.

After Leicester let him go, troubled striker Stan Collymore pitches up at Bradford City and scores a spectacular overhead kick on his debut in the Yorkshire derby against Leeds United.

"Carbone ... for COLLYMORE! Glorious goal! STAN IS BACK! AND HOW!"

Martin Tyler, Sky Sports commentator[5]

Leeds were also involved in the game of the season as they edged out Liverpool 4-3 in a thriller at Elland Road in November. The West Yorkshire club had their Australian striker Mark Viduka to thank for the victory – he netted all four of their goals.

> *"It was one of those games where every time I had a sniff of goal it went in. You very rarely get those kind of games but it was good to be a part of."*

A modest Mark Viduka in his post-match interview[6]

It was a busy time for the West Yorkshire club. As David O'Leary's young side continued to impress, they smashed the British transfer record, landing West Ham defender Rio Ferdinand for £18 million. It was an acquisition that would help Leeds reach the semi-final of the Champions League that season.

> **"It wasn't until I went to Leeds that my attitude began to change and mature – and my game really started to improve."**

Rio Ferdinand[7]

In early December, there's a new record for the Premier League's fastest ever goal as Tottenham's Ledley King nets against Bradford before most people have taken their seats. The goal is timed at an unfathomable 10 seconds.

Manchester United's continued success, both domestically and on the Continent, may have brought a glut of silverware to Old Trafford but it's also brought a new kind of fan to the Theatre of Dreams.

"Away from home our fans are fantastic, I'd call them the hardcore fans. But at home they have a few drinks and probably the prawn sandwiches, and they don't realise what's going on out on the pitch."

Roy Keane, Manchester United captain, lays waste to the changing nature of football fans at Old Trafford.[8]

As Christmas approached, there was an act of sportsmanship that showed a different side to the sport and, for that matter, to one of its more interesting characters, Paolo Di Canio. It was Everton v West Ham and the score was 1-1 when, late on, Everton goalkeeper Paul Gerrard collapsed with what later transpired to be a dislocated knee.

With Gerrard injured and unable to get to his feet, West Ham played on, but as the ball was crossed into the Toffees' area Di Canio simply caught it, rather than put it in the net, and summoned on the paramedics.

"Harry Redknapp was the West Ham manager at that time and by all accounts he was going absolutely ballistic after the game. The game was 1-1 and there was only a few minutes or so left at that point, so a goal probably would have won them the game."

Paul Gerrard, Everton keeper[9]

> *"Paolo has taken a lot of abuse for different things in his career, but he deserves great credit."*
>
> Walter Smith, Everton manager[10]

On 21 February, Arsenal visit Old Trafford – and return home on the wrong end of a 6-1 humiliation. It's a victory that gives United a colossal 16-point advantage over the Gunners. Many bookmakers have long since stopped taking bets on the Red Devils to win the Premier League and some have already paid out on United as league winners.

"United haven't done anything special this season."

Arsène Wenger does United's team talk for them ahead of the game at Old Trafford.[11]

"To score three goals in less than 22 minutes was amazing. I got out of bed on the right side that morning ... I just had one of those magical moments on the football pitch."

Dwight Yorke, United's man of the match, on the quick-fire hat trick that helped sink the Gunners.[12]

Four years after Alf-Inge Haaland had accused Keane of feigning injury during a game between Leeds and Manchester United, the Red Devils' Irish skipper exacted brutal revenge at Old Trafford with a high, straight red-card challenge that seriously injured the Norwegian's right knee. He retired in July 2003.

"I'll have to see whether any of Keane's studs are still in there."

Alf-Inge Haaland awaits the results of the scan on his injured knee.[13]

In the winter transfer window, Manchester United are linked with a move for West Ham's talismanic Italian Paolo Di Canio, but the move doesn't materialise.

"Di Canio would have been capable of becoming a truly great player at Manchester United ... we make heroes quickly here. Di Canio could have been in that category."

Manchester United manager Sir Alex Ferguson[14]

There were emotional scenes at The Dell on the final day of the season, where 103 years of history was about to end for Southampton and its supporters ahead of their move to a new stadium, St Mary's. And what a game to draw the curtain. Saints would run out 3-2 winners against Arsenal, with club legend Matt Le Tissier scoring a sensational half-volley on the turn in the last minute to seal the victory. It was fairy-tale stuff.

> ## "It's very special to score the last goal and I couldn't have imagined a better ending."
> Southampton hero Matt Le Tissier[15]

> ## "We did not intrude on their party – we gave them what they wanted in the last minute."
> Arsène Wenger, the ever-generous Arsenal manager.[16]

With five weeks to spare, United sealed the Premier League title with a 4-2 win over struggling Coventry City on Easter Sunday. That result, coupled with Arsenal's shock home defeat to Middlesbrough, saw United claim their seventh Premier League championship in the nine-year history of the competition.

It had been another championship cakewalk, another imperious masterclass. They could even afford to lose their final three games as Sir Alex Ferguson rang the changes and gave other squad members a game. They were that far ahead.

It was a less auspicious campaign for United's neighbours, Manchester City. After a four-year absence from the top flight, Joe Royle's team had won back-to-back promotions but had struggled throughout the season and had their relegation confirmed with a 2-1 defeat at Ipswich Town in their penultimate game.

> "Motivating players isn't easy when their first signing-on fee pays off their mortgage. There is great consolation in not playing and going home in a Porsche. In my day the car park was all Vivas and Cortinas."
> Joe Royle, Manchester City manager, on the problem with modern players. Royle would be sacked within days of City's relegation.[17]

After 34 successive seasons of top-flight football, Coventry City's stay in the highest division finally comes to an end. They finish in 19th place, eight points adrift of safety, one place ahead of rock-bottom Bradford City.

> ## "I'm in a state of stunned disappointment, I couldn't see that coming."
> Gordon Strachan, Coventry manager, on his first taste of relegation as a player or manager.[18]

It was an exceptional season for Liverpool. Though they finished third in the league, they had won a unique treble under their French manager, Gerard Houllier, taking the FA Cup, the League Cup and the UEFA Cup.

"Gerard put us back on the map in Europe with that UEFA Cup run in 2001. He was also the first manager to get us into the Champions League. The treble in 2001 is definitely under-appreciated. That season was unbelievable. To win a trophy in a season is a great thing. To win three?"

Jamie Carragher, former Liverpool defender and part of the treble-winning team.[19]

It's also a season to remember for Leeds United, as they finish fourth in the league and reach the semi-finals of the Champions League in a run that sees them beat AC Milan, Anderlecht and Lazio on their way to a last four defeat to Valencia.

But it was United's title once more, their third in a row. It made Sir Alex Ferguson the first manager in history to win three successive league titles with the same club. Within days of the end of the season, however, Ferguson dropped a bombshell – he would leave his post as Manchester United manager at the end of 2001/2 season, having steered the club to seven league titles, four FA Cup wins, one League Cup, a European Cup Winner' Cup and the Champions League in 1999.

It was the end of a golden era. Or was it?

"I will be leaving Manchester United at the end of the season and that is it."

Sir Alex Ferguson announces his intention to retire.[20]

And did Fergie get the Manager of the Year Award? No, that went to newly promoted Ipswich's George Burley, who had taken his team to an unlikely fifth-placed finish.

"Going into the season I'd thought if we'd finish fourth-bottom it would have been a fantastic season, so to finish fifth was unbelievable for the players and myself. It was something you could never have dreamed of."

George Burley, Manager of the Year[21]

Games Played: 38

Pos	Team	GD	Pts
1	Manchester United	+48	80
2	Arsenal	+25	70
3	Liverpool	+32	69
4	Leeds United	+21	68
5	Ipswich Town	+15	66
6	Chelsea	+23	61
7	Sunderland	+5	57
8	Aston Villa	+3	54
9	Charlton Athletic	-7	52
10	Southampton	-8	52
11	Newcastle United	-6	51
12	Tottenham Hotspur	-7	49
13	Leicester City	-12	48
14	Middlesbrough	0	42
15	West Ham United	-5	42
16	Everton	-14	42
17	Derby County	-22	42
18	Manchester City	-24	34
19	Coventry City	-27	34
20	Bradford City	-40	26

CHAMPIONS: Manchester United

RUNNERS-UP: Arsenal

RELEGATED: Manchester City, Coventry City, Bradford City

PROMOTED: Blackburn Rovers, Fulham, Bolton Wanderers

TOP GOALSCORER: Jimmy Floyd Hasselbaink, Chelsea – 23

PLAYER OF THE SEASON: Teddy Sheringham, Manchester United

MANAGER OF THE SEASON: George Burley, Ipswich

DID YOU KNOW? *George Burley's Manager of the Season award was the first time the award had gone to a manager who hadn't won the league in that season.*

PREMIER LEAGUE 2001/02

Global League

The 10th anniversary of the Premier League saw English clubs' progress in Europe rewarded with an additional Champions League place. Now there would be four berths up for grabs and the battle to win one would be more intense than ever. There's a new sponsor too, with Barclaycard taking over the mantle from Carling.

As a result, the Premier League clubs are busier than ever in the transfer market. Manchester United, for example, break the British transfer record to land Lazio's Argentinian midfielder Juan Sebastian Veron for £28.1 million and also spend £19 million on Ruud van Nistelrooy, finally landing the prolific Dutch striker a year after a proposed move collapsed because of a knee injury to the PSV forward.

In London, highly rated midfielder Frank Lampard leaves West Ham to join London rivals Chelsea in an £11 million deal, while Fulham pull off a coup of their own, signing Dutch international goalkeeper Edwin van der Sar for £7.1 million. Leeds snap up Inter Milan's Irish striker Robbie Keane and, later, Liverpool's Robbie Fowler.

By far the most controversial transfer of the summer window happens in north London, where out-of-contract England defender Sol Campbell snubs Tottenham's offer to make him the club's highest-paid player to join bitter rivals Arsenal on a four-year contract.

> **"People who were perhaps five at the time I went to Arsenal, or were not even born, feel strongly about it. Who is perpetuating this? It is incredible."**
>
> Sol Campbell, on how he still gets grief over the transfer to this day.[1]

Manchester City also have a new manager. Following Joe Royle's sacking at the end of the disappointing 2000/01 season, they turn to former England manager Kevin Keegan.

"They've gone for a top-class manager and they don't come any bigger than Kevin Keegan."

Paul Ritchie, City's defender[2]

> "He walked away from the Newcastle job, he walked away from the Fulham job and he walked away from the England job. We'll have to wait and see if he'll walk away from the Manchester City job."
>
> Rodney Marsh, former Manchester City star[3]

And, soon after the season starts, there are signs of unrest at Old Trafford as manager Sir Alex Ferguson sanctions the surprise sale of their star defender Jaap Stam to the Italian Serie A side Lazio. It's a shock development but one, in the wake of Stam publishing a controversial autobiography, that underlines Ferguson's determination to show just who's in charge at Old Trafford.

"It was a bolt from the blue. I didn't see it coming. I've never wanted to leave this club. I love it here."

Jaap Stam[4]

> *"At the time he had just come back from an Achilles injury and we thought he had just lost a little bit. We got the offer from Lazio, £16.5m for a centre-back who was 29. It was an offer I couldn't refuse. But in playing terms it was a mistake."*
>
> Sir Alex Ferguson, Manchester United manager[5]

The furore over Stam's book and his departure sees United off to an uncharacteristically indifferent start, registering just two wins in their opening five fixtures. There are no such issues for Arsenal, though, who despite a 2-1 home defeat to Leeds reach the top of the table by the end of September.

Yet reports of United's demise are greatly exaggerated, as a comeback of epic proportions against Tottenham at White Hart Lane at the end of September demonstrates. In a whirlwind first half, Spurs race into a 3-0 lead but it's a different story in the second 45 minutes as five answered goals from Andy Cole, Laurent Blanc, Ruud van Nistelrooy, Juan Sebastian Veron and David Beckham secure an astonishing win for the reigning champions.

> "I'm not saying exactly what I said to them at half time – why am I always asked that?"
>
> Sir Alex Ferguson, United manager[6]

"It was terrible because at halftime we thought we were one of the best teams in the league and by full time we felt like one of the worst."

Gus Poyet, Tottenham midfielder[7]

> "Gawd help the rest of us if they start keeping clean sheets."
>
> Glenn Hoddle, Spurs manager, fears for the rest of the Premier League.[8]

On the Hampshire coast, Southampton appoint Gordon Strachan as their new manager in the wake of Stuart Gray's short-lived tenure.

> *"I was asked if I thought I was the right man for the job and I said, 'No, I think they should have got George Graham because I'm useless.'"*
>
> Gordon Strachan's response when he's asked if he's up to the task of reviving Southampton's fortunes.[9]

In late October, after an unbeaten start to the season, Aston Villa's Peter Schmeichel becomes the first goalkeeper in Premiership history to score as he volleys home in stoppage time against Everton. His historic strike is in vain, however, as Villa fall to their first defeat of their campaign, going down 3-2 and missing the chance to go top of the table.

"I've seen goalkeepers score before on television, but never in a game that I've been managing. And I hope that I don't see it again. You watch Schmeichel come running up for these situations, he does it a lot. And you just keep your fingers crossed because you think it's going to be Sod's law."

Walter Smith, Everton manager[10]

There's relief in the red half of Manchester as Sir Alex Ferguson performs a U-turn and announces that he won't be retiring at the end of the season as planned. Instead, the 60-year-old signs a new three-year contract at United.

"The biggest mistake I made was announcing it at the start of the season. … They thought, 'Oh, the manager's leaving', but when I changed my mind in the January, I started thinking about United again and how we could get back on top."

Sir Alex Ferguson, Manchester United manager[11]

Come Christmas and it was Bobby Robson's Newcastle United that led the way, with impressive victories over title rivals Arsenal, Manchester United and Leeds.

"We're not quite a brilliant team yet but we're on the verge of becoming a brilliant team. We are a talented, fit, forceful team. We have no physical incapabilities, we're winning at the end of matches."

Bobby Robson, Newcastle manager[12]

It wouldn't be long before Newcastle's striker and captain, Alan Shearer, scored his 200th goal in the Premiership, lashing home a late goal to help the Magpies to a 3-0 win against Charlton and all but confirm Newcastle's place in the Champions League the following season.

"I can't tell you how delighted I was when it hit the back of the net. The reception I received from the fans was something I'll never forget, and I was delighted to do it in front of my people, if you like."

Alan Shearer[13]

Though they had been challenging Newcastle at the top end of the table, Leeds United's form in the second half of the season saw them lose ground in the race for the Champions League places. Their failure to make the top four – they would finish in fifth place, five points adrift of Newcastle United – would not only see the club plunge into an existential crisis but also prompt the departure of manager David O'Leary, who, after four years in charge and having spent over £100 million on players, was unceremoniously sacked in June 2002.

> **"I went in to clear a few things up before I went on holiday and I got the sack."**
>
> David O'Leary, former Newcastle United manager[14]

"We lived the dream."

Peter Ridsdale, Leeds chairman, the man who green-lighted Leeds' massive overspending.[15]

Meanwhile in Manchester, United boss Alex Ferguson goes on the attack as the press question the form of his Argentinian international, Juan Sebastian Veron.

> **"He [Veron] is a f****** great player and you're all f****** idiots."**
>
> Sir Alex Ferguson, Manchester United manager[16]

At the foot of the table, Leicester City are relegated by the beginning of April as they lose 1-0 to Manchester United. They do salvage some pride, however, by winning their last ever game at their Filbert Street home as they defeat Spurs 2-1. They will start life in their new 32,000 all-seater stadium in the First Division.

> **"I'm sad we haven't been able to stay in the Premier League … The fact that the crowd were in good voice at the end of this tough game was a tremendous show of unity. It augurs well for the future of Leicester City Football Club."**
>
> Dave Bassett, Leicester City manager[17]

The Foxes would be joined by East Midlands' rivals Derby County and Ipswich Town in dropping down a division. For Ipswich especially, it was, in every sense of the word, a rollercoaster of a season. Though they were playing in the UEFA Cup, they had won only one of their first 17 games before going on a run of seven wins from eight matches. But they couldn't maintain that form and just one win from their final 17 games saw them relegated in 18th place, with the final nail in the Tractor Boys' coffin coming in a 5-0 final day defeat against Liverpool.

"We have been victims of our own success. Our eyes were on Europe back in August and we never identified a realistic target for this season. The consolation is that we are stronger now than we have ever been before. Our target has to be to win the First Division."

David Sheepshanks, Ipswich Town chairman[18]

With two games to play, and just four days after they had beaten Chelsea in the FA Cup final, Arsenal travelled to Old Trafford knowing that a draw would see them become only the second team in history to have won the double on three occasions. United, meanwhile, needed a win to take the title to the final day.

But it would be Arsenal's day – and season. Thanks to a second-half Sylvain Wiltord goal, the Gunners took all three points, ending United's three-season stranglehold on the Premier League title.

"Hand it over, Ferguson!"

Arsenal fans demand their silverware at Old Trafford[19]

"I certainly don't begrudge them their share of honours because they play the game the right way."

Faint praise from Sir Alex Ferguson[20]

"Everyone thinks they have the prettiest wife at home."

Arsène Wenger, Arsenal's manager, responds to Ferguson's claim that United had played the better football in the Premier League that season.[21]

Their final game, a 4-3 win over Everton at Highbury, meant that the Gunners had won their final 13 games (equalling the league record) and they had scored in every game in the league season as they stormed to their second Premier League title. It was the perfect send-off for half of the most formidable back four in the competition's history as Tony Adams and Lee Dixon hung up their boots.

> **"The greatest Arsenal man of all time. ... I don't think anyone has represented the club from the age of 17 to 35 and sustained all the injuries he's had, while half the time fighting for his own soul. Only those close to him knew how bad it was."**
>
> Arsenal legend Bob Wilson pays tribute to Tony Adams.[22]

Games Played: 38

Pos	Team	GD	Pts
1	Arsenal	+43	87
2	Liverpool	+37	80
3	Manchester United	+42	77
4	Newcastle United	+22	71
5	Leeds United	+16	66
6	Chelsea	+28	64
7	West Ham United	−9	53
8	Aston Villa	−1	50
9	Tottenham Hotspur	−4	50
10	Blackburn Rovers	+4	46
11	Southampton	−8	45
12	Middlesbrough	−12	45
13	Fulham	−8	44
14	Charlton Athletic	−11	44
15	Everton	−12	43
16	Bolton Wanderers	−18	40
17	Sunderland	−22	40
18	Ipswich Town	−23	36
19	Derby County	−30	30
20	Leicester City	-34	28

CHAMPIONS: Arsenal

RUNNERS-UP: Liverpool

RELEGATED: Ipswich Town, Derby County, Leicester City

PROMOTED: Manchester City, Birmingham City, West Bromwich Albion

TOP GOALSCORER: Thierry Henry, Arsenal – 24

PLAYER OF THE SEASON: Freddie Ljungberg, Arsenal

MANAGER OF THE SEASON: Arsène Wenger, Arsenal

DID YOU KNOW? *Newcastle United won 34 points from losing positions in 2001/2 – the most by a team in a single Premier League season.*

PREMIER LEAGUE 2002/03

Living the Dream

In the 10 years since the Premier League had come into being, it had become a phenomenon unlike any other in modern-day sport. Attendances were up across the board, the revenues from the sale of broadcasting rights now ran into the billions of pounds and the players' salaries had grown concomitantly.

Put simply, the English top flight had become *the* place to play and watch football.

Inevitably, the transfer fees were also reaching unheralded levels. On 22 July, Manchester United smash the British transfer record by paying £29 million for Leeds United's central defender Rio Ferdinand, just 18 months after Leeds had done the same to buy him and days after the Leeds chairman, Peter Ridsdale, insisted he wasn't for sale.

"The only thing that I can confirm is that if Rio Ferdinand hands in a transfer request it will be turned down. He is going nowhere. Where does he think he is going? Into thin air?"

Peter Ridsdale, Leeds United chairman[1]

'Despite what some people think, we have every right to improve ourselves.'

Sir Alex Ferguson, Manchester United manager[2]

When the season begins, Arsenal pick up where they left off from their double-winning season and break the record of 13 consecutive wins in the top flight as they beat Birmingham City 2-0. The streak ends the following week when they come from two goals down to take a point against West Ham.

But it's merely a blip. The Gunners win seven of their first nine games and play the kind of football that has the opposition chasing shadows. A case in point is the game against Leeds at the end of September where Arsenal blow the home side away, winning 4-1.

79

"We're all fighting for second place now. It was demoralising. They just pass and move, pass and move. You find yourself working for nothing."

Olivier Dacourt, Leeds United's French midfielder[3]

> **"Manchester United have been exceptional for 10 years – but I've not seen anything as good as that."**
>
> And Terry Venables, the Leeds manager[4]

"We are playing great, 'Total Football'. Danger comes from everywhere."

Arsène Wenger, Arsenal manager[5]

Arsenal's seemingly irrepressible march towards back-to-back titles hits the buffers, albeit briefly, in October when they travel to Goodison Park to play Everton on the back of a 30-match unbeaten run. The game is poised at 1-1 going into the last minute. Enter 16-year-old local lad Wayne Rooney, who picks the ball up 35 yards out, turns, and drives towards goal. As he's closed down he unleashes all manner of hell on the ball and it dips and swerves and crashes in off the underside of the crossbar, leaving the ponytailed Arsenal keeper David Seaman clutching thin air. Not only does the wonder goal win the match for Everton but it makes Rooney the youngest goalscorer in Premier League history.

A star is born.

"Remember the name ... Wayne Rooney!"

Clive Tyldesley, ITV commentator[6]

"It wasn't a case of if Wayne Rooney was going to make it, but when. We'd got used to him doing ridiculous things in training so it wasn't a shock to us that he could score a goal like that against Arsenal."

David Unsworth, Rooney's Everton teammate[7]

Arsenal's only challengers in the opening months of the campaign were Liverpool. Gerard Houllier's side would enjoy a 12-match unbeaten run from the start of the season, a run that would include seven wins on the spin and victories over Manchester City, Chelsea, Leeds and Spurs. But after a 1-0 defeat at Middlesbrough on 9 November, they fell into an 11-match winless slide that rendered that start meaningless. It's the Reds' worst top-flight run for 80 years.

"If the title dream wasn't dead already, it was smelling a bit funny before this defeat. Now the ceremonial burial of Premiership aspirations can be arranged."

After a 1-0 defeat away to Newcastle on New Year's Day, the *Liverpool Echo* has its say.[8]

There were struggles aplenty at Sunderland too, where, having gained just eight points from their first nine games, they decide to part company with manager Peter Reid. He is replaced by Howard Wilkinson, the man who had guided Leeds United to the title over 10 years earlier and who had been the FA's Technical Director.

"While I know that the recent months have been difficult and disappointing that should not cloud people's judgement over the many positive things Peter has achieved for the club over many years."

Sunderland chairman Bob Murray's statement.[9]

November also saw the last ever Manchester derby at City's Maine Road. The ground had been home to Manchester City for 80 years and Kevin Keegan's newly promoted side would give the famous old stadium the send-off it deserved, winning 3-1, with Shaun Goater capitalising on a calamitous error from Gary Neville to score one of his two goals.

"GARY NEVILLE IS A BLUE!"

City's fans have a new chant.[10]

"My greatest derby."

City boss Kevin Keegan on his club's first win over United in 17 attempts.[11]

> *"I've given them a bollocking, and quite rightly."*

Sir Alex Ferguson, less than enamoured with United's performance.[12]

Fergie's 'hairdryer treatment' worked — but then it usually did. United won four of their next five matches, comfortably beating Liverpool and Arsenal in the process. But Fergie still wasn't happy. After a poor performance in the FA Cup, the United boss had read the riot act in the dressing room and kicked a football boot straight into the face of David Beckham, cutting him above the eye. It's Beckham's final season with the club.

> **"There are no hard feelings from me about the boot in the face thing. It was forgotten straight away..."**

David Beckham[13]

With just two wins from 20 league games in his five months in charge and Sunderland rock bottom of the Premier League, March sees the end of the road for Black Cats' boss Howard Wilkinson. The nadir of his tenure comes in a 3-1 defeat at Charlton, where his team contrives to score three own goals in just seven first-half minutes. Though Mick McCarthy is drafted in, he can't save Sunderland and they are relegated with a record league low total of 19 points. It's hardly surprising. After all, they did lose their last 15 games in succession.

> "It's nice to be here, it's a privilege actually. It's a wonderful club, a proper football club. Everything about the club is right except results."

Mick McCarthy, the new Sunderland manager[14]

With nine games to play, Arsenal enjoy a healthy eight-point lead over Manchester United but a 2-0 away defeat at Blackburn allows the Red Devils to claw back some ground.

> **"It's getting tickly now – squeaky-bum time, I call it. It's going to be an interesting few weeks and the standard of the Premiership is such that nothing will be easy."**

Sir Alex Ferguson, with a remark that would go down in history.[15]

Arsenal begin to crack, winning just once in April as United take full advantage, bagging 13 points. When Ferguson's team beat Spurs 2-0 on 26 April, they open up a five-point lead over Arsenal, and when the Gunners lose 3-2 at home to Leeds in early May, United have one hand on the trophy.

In their last eight games, United win seven times, scoring 26 goals, with their Dutch striker Ruud Van Nistelrooy grabbing half of them. He ends the season with 25 league goals and 44 in all competitions, earning him the season's Golden Boot award.

It's the kind of form that Arsenal can't live with and United coast to victory, eventually winning their eighth Premier League title by a comfortable five points. It's a remarkable turnaround for United, especially as they had won just eight points from their first six games – their worst tally since 1989/90.

> "I never doubt United. I know (the players') capabilities.
> When you are with a group for a long time you know them."
>
> Sir Alex Ferguson, Manchester United manager.[16]

> *"We lost to a team that spend 50% more than we do."*
>
> Arsène Wenger, the ever-gracious Arsenal manager[17]

For West Ham, it's a cruel end to the season. With 42 points, they have been relegated with the highest points total in the history of the Premier League. They will go on to be labelled as one of the best teams ever to go down.

"[We] had England internationals ... How we took that team into the Championship is beyond me. That team should have been easily competing for top six, top seven. To this day it's still a mystery how we went down."

Don Hutchison, West Ham midfielder[18]

Games Played: 38

Pos	Team	GD	Pts
1	Manchester United	+40	83
2	Arsenal	+43	78
3	Newcastle United	+15	69
4	Chelsea	+30	67
5	Liverpool	+20	64
6	Blackburn Rovers	+9	60
7	Everton	-1	59
8	Southampton	-3	52
9	Manchester City	-7	51
10	Tottenham Hotspur	-11	50
11	Middlesbrough	+4	49
12	Charlton Athletic	-11	49
13	Birmingham City	-8	48
14	Fulham	-9	48
15	Leeds United	+1	47
16	Aston Villa	-5	45
17	Bolton Wanderers	-10	44
18	West Ham United	-17	42
19	West Bromwich Albion	-36	26
20	Sunderland	-44	19

CHAMPIONS: Manchester United

RUNNERS-UP: Arsenal

RELEGATED: West Ham United, West Bromwich Albion, Sunderland

PROMOTED: Portsmouth, Leicester City, Wolverhampton Wanderers

TOP GOALSCORER: Ruud Van Nistelrooy, Manchester United – 25

PLAYER OF THE SEASON: Thierry Henry, Arsenal

MANAGER OF THE SEASON: Sir Alex Ferguson, Manchester United

DID YOU KNOW? *Sunderland's 15–game losing streak in 2002/3 would become a record 20-match streak when they returned to the Premier League in 2005/6 and lost their first five games of the season.*

PREMIER LEAGUE 2003/04

Unbeaten. Unrivalled.
Invincible.

The summer of 2003 sees a sea change in the way that top-flight football in England operates as the Russian billionaire Roman Abramovich buys Chelsea Football Club for £140 million. With a personal wealth estimated at £8 billion, the 36-year-old arrives in London determined to build a team that could challenge on both domestic and European fronts. Certainly, he has the cash to do it.

"I created the Chelsea miracle from nothing and my achievement convinced Abramovich to buy the club."

Chelsea manager Claudio Ranieri claims the credit.[1]

True to his word, Abramovich immediately begins using his vast resources to bolster Chelsea's squad. In came Glen Johnson (£6 million), the Real Madrid star Geremi (£7 million), Wayne Bridge (£7 million), Damien Duff (£17 million), Joe Cole (£6.6 million), Juan Sebastian Veron (£15 million), Adrian Mutu (£15 million), Alexei Smertin (£3.45 million), Hernan Crespo (£17 million) and, the icing on the cake, Real Madrid's classy midfielder Claude Makelele (£16 million). And all of this in less than two months.

"Just when transfer fees were reacquainting themselves with reality, a Russian billionaire has sent them back into orbit like oil from a sabotaged well."

Paul Hayward, *The Daily Telegraph*[2]

There was also change afoot at Manchester United as David Beckham, his star in the ascendant, left for pastures new in a £25 million move to Real Madrid. In his place comes a spotty 18-year-old from Madeira, Portugal, Cristiano Ronaldo. He joins the Old Trafford club for £12.24 million, becoming the most expensive teenager in English football history. He's also given the number seven shirt, the same number worn by United legends like George Best, Eric Cantona and the departing David Beckham.

> **"I'm especially proud to be the first Portuguese player to join United and I'm looking forward to helping the team achieve even more success."**
>
> Cristiano Ronaldo[3]

> *"At that age Ronaldo is not just a footballer, he is waiting to be an icon. He would enhance any team, any league anywhere. I really believe he is that good."*
>
> Prophetic words from the Portuguese legend Eusebio.[4]

It didn't take long for Ronaldo to display his potential. On the opening day of the season, against Bolton Wanderers, he creates three goals as a second-half substitute as United dispatch Sam Allardyce's side 4-0 at Old Trafford.

"It was a marvellous debut, almost unbelievable."

Sir Alex Ferguson, Manchester United manager[5]

> "He reminds me of Ryan Giggs when he first started – he can go inside, outside, uses both feet and runs at people. Everyone holds their breath when he gets the ball."
>
> Sam Allardyce, Bolton boss[6]

Young Ronaldo must have wondered just what he'd got himself into just a few weeks later, though, when Arsenal visit Old Trafford and one of the most intense, volatile and sometimes violent encounters between these two rivals takes place. It would even become known as 'The Battle of Old Trafford'.

The tackles fly in, there are bookings galore, Arsenal captain Patrick Vieira is sent off and when United's Ruud Van Nistelrooy misses a last-minute penalty, the Arsenal defender Martin Keown leaps in front of him, goading him relentlessly.

"My behaviour was not acceptable from an Arsenal point of view, but you can't take that back. I rang my wife after the game, and she's usually very supportive, but she said 'I think you've gone and done it now'. It was the first time she'd ever said anything like that."

Martin Keown, Arsenal defender[7]

"The truth is, I wasn't aware because I was so gutted about missing the penalty. I couldn't care less what they were doing. I was in shock, thinking 'I missed, I missed'."

United's Ruud Van Nistelrooy[8]

"A mob who get away with murder."

Sir Alex Ferguson, Manchester United manager[9]

Despite the huge influx of new players at Chelsea, manager Claudio Ranieri manages to foster a genuine team spirit among his league of nations squad. The Blues are unbeaten in their opening eight games, winning six. But as the world's sports media continue to focus on the seismic shift in power at Stamford Bridge, it's Arsenal, with new signings Cesc Fabregas, Gael Clichy and German goalkeeper Jens Lehmann in their ranks, that provide their only real opposition.

The two sides meet at Highbury on 18 October and after early goals from Edu for the Gunners and Hernan Crespo for Chelsea, it's left to Thierry Henry to seize on a Carlo Cudicini fumble to pinch the points.

But it's not going so well at rivals Spurs where, after two and a half years in charge, and despite being one of the finest players ever to wear the Spurs shirt, manager Glenn Hoddle is sacked on 21 September. His team are third from bottom with just four points from six matches. He is replaced by Director of Football David Pleat until the end of the season.

"Unfortunately the start to this season has been our worst since the Premiership was formed ... It is critical that I, and the board, have absolute confidence in the manager to deliver success to the club. Regrettably we do not."

Daniel Levy, Tottenham chairman[10]

As Leeds United's debts spiral to £100 million and with no money to invest in players, it's almost inevitable that they struggle in the Premier League. As they collect just eight points from their first 12 games, it's manager Peter Reid who carries the can, with a 6-1 defeat to Portsmouth being the final nail in his coffin.

"There was no one in my team today who realised the situation we're in. They don't deserve to pick up their wage packets."

Peter Reid after the humiliation at Portsmouth, the club's worst defeat since 1959.[11]

"There's been a fall from grace – we've got to try and pick that up ... The club spent money they didn't have. That's why they are in the position they are in today."

The new caretaker manager at Leeds, former player Eddie Gray.[12]

As Leeds head south, Arsenal continue on a run that takes them all the way to Christmas undefeated. Nobody can beat them and, more to the point, they are playing the kind of football that suggests nobody will.

"This is the closest I have seen to the Dutch idea of total football. They can all play one-touch football and if you have that throughout your team, it's unstoppable."

Dennis Bergkamp, Arsenal striker[13]

"Arsenal caress a football the way I dreamed of caressing Marilyn Monroe."

Brian Clough, former Nottingham Forest manager[14]

Just a week before Christmas, Manchester United's title defence is dealt a severe blow when their central defender Rio Ferdinand is banned for eight months and fined £50,000 for missing a drugs test earlier in the season. The sentence means he misses the rest of the Premier League season and England's participation in the European Championships that summer.

Desperate to add some more firepower to their ranks, Manchester United sign Fulham's Louis Saha in the January transfer window. The French striker had scored 13 goals in the first half of the season and attracts widespread interest.

"I remember playing against him as a centre-back when he was at Fulham and he destroyed me three seasons on the bounce. I was devastated when I had to play against him and I thought 'we've got to sign him'."

Gary Neville, Manchester United's full-back[15]

The new year sees Arsenal embark on a run of nine consecutive wins that all but puts paid to the title race. It starts with a 4-1 rout of Middlesbrough and ends with a 1-1 draw with Manchester United at Highbury. In the following game, the Gunners get back to winning ways, coming from behind to beat Liverpool 4-2 with a Thierry Henry hat trick proving the difference. It's a pivotal win after a week that had seen them lose the FA Cup semi-final to Manchester United and to Chelsea in the quarter-finals of the Champions League and answers those critics who felt the Gunners were about to crumble.

"Thierry Henry was supposed to have a bad back but hit a hattrick that brought sunshine and laughter flooding back into Highbury again. Crisis? What crisis?"

Henry Winter, *The Telegraph*[16]

Despite a small upturn in results under Eddie Gray, Leeds United's relegation to the second tier is confirmed on 2 May when they go down 4-1 to Bolton Wanderers. It ends an 11-year stay in the top flight and comes just three years after they reached the Champions League semi-final.

"I'm realistic enough to know that, over the season, we weren't good enough. Nobody has a divine right. It will not be the end of the club."

Eddie Gray, Leeds manager. He would be replaced with Kevin Blackwell soon after the end of the season.[17]

At the happier end of the table sit Arsenal. Still unbeaten after 33 games, they wrap up the title at White Hart Lane, the same ground where they won the old First Division in the double-winning season of 1971. A 2-2 draw proves sufficient as Chelsea lose to Newcastle and have to make do with a runners-up spot.

> *"Even though we didn't win the game people will remember that we won the title at White Hart Lane ... We know it's special for the fans so you can't just leave and go home. They deserved it."*
>
> Thierry Henry explains his team's enthusiastic celebrations[18]

"My target now is to keep the players focused on our unbeaten record. We have put so much effort into this season so to lose a game now because we had switched off would not be ideal. We have to keep going."

Arsène Wenger, Arsenal manager[19]

The Gunners go into the final game of the 38-game season needing to avoid defeat against Leicester City at Highbury to create history.

It doesn't start well. A goal down at halftime, they draw level thanks to a Thierry Henry penalty, but when Patrick Vieira puts them ahead just after the hour there's no way the Gunners are going to lose.

Played 38. Won 26. Drew 12. Lost none.

They called them 'The Invincibles' and with good reason.

For the first and only time in the Premier League era and only the second time in the history of the top flight, Arsenal go the entire campaign unbeaten, romping to the league title by a massive 11 points.

> **"As long as you believe, then it is possible. It's a fantastic moment. I always had that dream and to fulfil it is marvellous."**
>
> Arsène Wenger, Arsenal manager[20]

Games Played: 38

Pos	Team	GD	Pts
1	Arsenal	+47	90
2	Chelsea	+37	79
3	Manchester United	+29	75
4	Liverpool	+18	60
5	Newcastle United	+12	56
6	Aston Villa	+4	56
7	Charlton Athletic	0	53
8	Bolton Wanderers	-8	53
9	Fulham	+6	52
10	Birmingham City	-5	50
11	Middlesbrough	-8	48
12	Southampton	-1	47
13	Portsmouth	-7	45
14	Tottenham Hotspur	-10	45
15	Blackburn Rovers	-8	44
16	Manchester City	+1	41
17	Everton	-12	39
18	Leicester City	-17	33
19	Leeds United	-39	33
20	Wolverhampton Wanderers	-39	33

CHAMPIONS: Arsenal

RUNNERS-UP: Chelsea

RELEGATED: Leicester City, Leeds United, Wolverhampton Wanderers

PROMOTED: West Bromwich Albion, Crystal Palace, Norwich City

TOP GOALSCORER: Thierry Henry, Arsenal – 30

PLAYER OF THE SEASON: Thierry Henry, Arsenal

MANAGER OF THE SEASON: Arsène Wenger, Arsenal

DID YOU KNOW? *For the first and only time in the history of the Premier League, all three relegated teams finished with the same number of points (33).*

Take it to the Bridge

A new sponsor and The Barclays Premiership title, it seemed, was Arsenal's to lose. The reigning champions had gone the entire 2003/4 season unbeaten and had, despite rampant transfer speculation, managed to hold on to their inspirational captain, Patrick Vieira.

Elsewhere in the division, Liverpool had a new manager with Valencia's Rafa Benitez filling the vacancy left by Gerard Houllier. Benitez would have to cope without the striking services of Michael Owen, however. The England striker seals a move to Spanish giants Real Madrid in August and is given the number 11 shirt made famous by the legendary Alfredo di Stefano.

"I am so proud to be wearing the number 11 shirt and I'd like to thank everyone for making me so welcome here. I would like to say a special thank you for being given the opportunity to play for the best team in the world."

Michael Owen[1]

Tottenham, meanwhile, hire Jaques Santini, fresh from guiding the French national team to the quarter-finals of that summer's European Championship. He would last just 13 games.

But the biggest and by far the most intriguing appointment came in west London, where Chelsea's new owner, the Russian oligarch Roman Abramovich, had appointed José Mourinho as the Blues' new boss.

Having led unfancied Porto to back-to-back league titles and the UEFA Cup and Champions League in successive seasons, the Portuguese was the most sought-after manager in the modern game.

And now here he was at Stamford Bridge, entertaining a rapt media corps…

"Please do not call me arrogant because what I say is true. I'm European champion ... I think I'm a special one!"

José Mourinho blows his own trumpet at his first press conference as the new Chelsea manager.[2]

After some stellar showings for England in the 2004 European Championships, Manchester United sign Everton's 18-year-old star Wayne Rooney for £25.6 million at the end of August 2004. It's the highest transfer fee ever paid for a teenager.

"I'm excited to be joining a club as big as Manchester United. I feel this can only improve my career."

Wayne Rooney, who would make his United debut in the Champions League against Fenerbache on 28 September, scoring a hat trick in a 6-2 win.[3]

"I think we have got the best young player this country has seen in the past 30 years."

High praise indeed from United manager Sir Alex Ferguson.[4]

The season begins on Saturday 14 August 2004.

A 5-3 win over Middlesbrough on the second weekend of the season saw Arsène Wenger's Arsenal equal Nottingham Forest's English record of 42 top-flight matches unbeaten. The Gunners would set the early pace in the division, winning eight of their opening nine fixtures.

A week later, just four games into the new season, Newcastle United dismissed legendary coach Sir Bobby Robson after five years at the helm at St. James' Park and having taken the Magpies to fifth place in the Premiership the previous season. Replaced by Graeme Souness, Newcastle would end the season in a disappointing 14th place – and Souness would be gone within 18 months.

"I am massively disappointed not to be able to finish the job I came here to do ... At the present moment, I have absolutely nothing to say except to thank the Geordie fans for their tremendous enthusiasm, loyalty and support."

Sir Bobby Robson can barely contain his frustration.[5]

Though Arsenal were leading the way, Chelsea had responded well to José Mourinho's management, winning four of their first five games and drawing the other.

On 19 September, Spurs visited Stamford Bridge with a clear strategy of just how to neutralise the threat from José Mourinho's flourishing Chelsea side. Their ultra-defensive tactics worked and the game ended goalless.

"As we say in Portugal, they brought the bus and they left the bus in front of the goal. ... There was only one team looking to win, they only came not to concede – it's not fair for the football we played."

A less than impressed José Mourinho, Chelsea manager.[6]

In October, Arsenal travelled to Old Trafford looking to make it a half century of games undefeated. It was a typically feisty encounter, with tackles flying in all over the pitch and referee Mike Riley struggling to keep the peace.

And it didn't end at the final whistle.

As United ran out 2-0 winners, the teams departed down the tunnel and as they reached the dressing rooms, it all kicked off.

"WHO HIT SIR ALEX WITH PIZZA?"

The *London Evening Standard*'s headline[7]

"The next thing I knew I had pizza all over me. ... I have no idea who the culprit was."

Sir Alex Ferguson, Manchester United manager[8]

Within weeks, United would also lose their inspirational skipper, Roy Keane, as the two parties, their relationship deteriorating, agreed to go their own ways. He joined Celtic soon after.

> **"I shed a few tears in my car outside the training ground for about two minutes."**
>
> Roy Keane, on the day he left United.[9]

Though the season was progressing better than anybody could have expected, there was some trouble ahead for Chelsea. Their Romanian striker Adrian Mutu had failed a drugs test in September. A month later, Chelsea terminated his contract.

> **"We want to make clear that Chelsea has a zero tolerance policy towards drugs. This applies to both performance-enhancing drugs or so-called 'recreational' drugs. They have no place at our club or in sport."**
>
> Chelsea FC statement[10]

North London derbies are never dull but on 13 November Spurs and Arsenal played out one of the all-time classics, with the Gunners edging their rivals 5-4 in a nine-goal classic.

> **"I've never played in a game like it – at least, not since I was a kid."**
>
> Ashley Cole[11]

But not everyone was enamoured with the game…

> **"That is not a proper football score; it is an ice hockey result."**
>
> José Mourinho, Chelsea manager[12]

The national sports press couldn't get enough of José Mourinho and his opinions on anything and everything. Throughout the season, the Chelsea boss was never far away from another back-page (and occasionally a front-page) headline.

In January 2005, for example, Mourinho had questioned why Manchester United manager Sir Alex Ferguson could speak to referees at halftime without censure from the authorities.

"I respect Sir Alex a lot because he's a great manager, but he must follow the procedure ... After the game on Wednesday we were together in my office and we spoke and drank wine. Unfortunately it was a very bad bottle of wine and he was complaining, so when we go to Old Trafford for the second leg, on my birthday, I will take a beautiful bottle of Portuguese wine."

Chelsea manager José Mourinho who, two weeks later, shared a bottle of 1964 vintage Barca Velha, worth £260, with his United counterpart. Lesson learned.[13]

> **"He was certainly full of it, calling me 'boss' and 'big man' when we had our post-match drink. But it would help if his greetings were accompanied by a decent glass of wine. What he gave me was paint-stripper."**
>
> ...and Sir Alex Ferguson agrees[14]

But that's not to say United aren't getting the rub of the green. Against Tottenham at Old Trafford there's a 50-yard shot from the visitors' Pedro Mendes that's dropped by Manchester United keeper, Roy Carroll. The ball crosses the goal-line by as much as a yard but the 'goal' isn't given by referee Mark Clattenburg. The game ends 0-0 and Spurs are deprived of three valuable points.

> **"It was a very nice goal, it was clearly over the line – I've never seen one so over the line and not given in my career. It's really, really over. What can you do but laugh about it?"**
>
> Pedro Mendes[15]

"I pride myself on being fast over a short distance but when the ball landed I was still 25 yards from goal and it was impossible to judge if it had crossed the line."

Rob Lewis, linesman[16]

Having enjoyed a five-point lead at Christmas, Chelsea had embarked on a run of eight straight victories, giving them an almost unassailable lead going into February.

It was a run made all the more remarkable by the fact that they didn't even concede a goal in any of those games, helping Blues' keeper Petr Cech eclipse Peter Schmeichel's Premier League record of 694 minutes without conceding.

"We are on top at the moment but not because of the club's financial power. We are in contention for a lot of trophies because of my hard work."

José Mourinho, never one to take the credit himself.[17]

Across London, Arsène Wenger was busy fielding the first entirely foreign 16-man squad in English football history with Ashley Cole ill and Sol Campbell injured. The team he eventually put out against Crystal Palace featured six Frenchmen, three Spaniards, two Dutchmen, one Cameroonian, one German, one Ivory Coast international, one Brazilian and a Swiss national.

> "I didn't know about that until I was told about it. I don't look at the passport of people, I look at their quality and their attitude."
>
> Arsène Wenger, Arsenal manager[18]

Meanwhile, on a chilly evening in East Anglia…

> *"A message for the best football supporters in the world. We need a 12th man here! Where are you? Where are you? Let's be 'avin' you! COME ON!"*
>
> Television chef and Norwich City shareholder Delia Smith attempts to rouse the Carrow Road crowd during their match against Manchester City. Well, Norwich lost 3-2 and went on to be relegated.[19]

In mid-March, Manchester City announced the departure of manager Kevin Keegan. The former England captain had informed the club of his decision to retire at the end of the 2005/6 season but the two parties had concluded it was best he went sooner rather than later.

He was replaced by Stuart Pearce.

"Manchester City announces that by mutual agreement our manager Kevin Keegan will leave the club with immediate effect. We all believe this is in the best interests of the club. Kevin's professionalism, infectious enthusiasm and drive for success have benefited all areas of the club."

Manchester City club statement[20]

In April, Newcastle United players Lee Bowyer and Kieron Dyer come to blows during their defeat at home to Aston Villa. Both men were red-carded, with Bowyer receiving a total ban of six games, a fine of £30,000 from the FA and a fine of six weeks' wages from his club. Dyer, meanwhile, received a three-match ban.

> *"When you play football, you have to be that way. You have to want to win. Sometimes it goes too far – that's what happened that day."*
>
> Lee Bowyer[21]

"I still see him now, we are friends. That's just the way Lee was. But I still want to beat him up."

Kieron Dyer[22]

As ever, Arsenal finished the season strongly, winning eight of their final 10 games to take second place, six points ahead of Manchester United in third. It included a 7-0 drubbing of Everton in their penultimate game.

> "No criticism of the players but tonight as a manager I'm totally embarrassed with what happened."
>
> David Moyes, Everton's manager, reflects on the Toffees' heaviest defeat since 1949.[23]

Despite being bottom of the table and eight points adrift of safety on Christmas Day, West Bromwich Albion pulled off a miraculous escape on the final day, the so-called 'Survival Sunday', leaving Southampton, Crystal Palace and Norwich relegated.

> **"This is the best ever. It is a fantastic feeling. The lads have done me proud and worked their socks off. They deserve this."**
>
> Bryan Robson, Baggies' manager, revels in a moment to savour.[24]

With just one defeat all campaign (away at Manchester City), a record number of points collected (95) and the fewest goals ever conceded in a Premier League season (15), Chelsea, under new manager José Mourinho, had stormed to their first title in 50 years.

They had also won the League Cup and, having beaten the likes of Paris St Germain, Barcelona, Bayern Munich and Mourinho's old club Porto, reached the semi-finals of the Champions League, only to be edged out by Liverpool, who go on to win the event, coming from three goals down to beat AC Milan on penalties.

Mourinho's – and Roman Abramovich's – Stamford Bridge revolution had lift-off…

"This is the start of a process not the end. I want more for me and Chelsea."

José Mourinho, Chelsea manager[25]

Games Played: 38

Pos	Team	GD	Pts
1	Chelsea	+57	95
2	Arsenal	+51	83
3	Manchester United	+32	77
4	Everton	-1	61
5	Liverpool	+11	58
6	Bolton Wanderers	+5	58
7	Middlesbrough	+7	55
8	Manchester City	+8	52
9	Tottenham Hotspur	+6	52
10	Aston Villa	-7	47
11	Charlton Athletic	-16	46
12	Birmingham City	-6	45
13	Fulham	-8	44
14	Newcastle United	-10	44
15	Blackburn Rovers	-11	42
16	Portsmouth	-16	39
17	West Bromwich Albion	-25	34
18	Crystal Place	-21	33
19	Norwich City	-35	33
20	Southampton	-21	32

CHAMPIONS: Chelsea

RUNNERS-UP: Arsenal

RELEGATED: Crystal Palace, Norwich City, Southampton

PROMOTED: West Ham United, Wigan Athletic, Sunderland

TOP GOALSCORER: Thierry Henry, Arsenal – 25

PLAYER OF THE SEASON: John Terry, Chelsea

MANAGER OF THE SEASON: José Mourinho, Chelsea

DID YOU KNOW? *Chelsea's 29 wins in the 2004/5 season was also a Premier League record.*

PREMIER LEAGUE 2005/06

Highs and Lows

As football took a back seat to England's Ashes-winning cricket team, the nation's clubs nevertheless busied themselves in the transfer market, wheeling and dealing with some high-profile moves taking place. Patrick Vieira, for example, ended nine years at Arsenal as he completed a £13.7 million move to Juventus; Liverpool snapped up Southampton's Peter Crouch for £7 million; and Phil Neville swapped Old Trafford for Goodison after 12 years at Manchester United.

Champions Chelsea, meanwhile, wasted no time in bolstering their squad ahead of their title defence, signing Manchester City's Shaun Wright-Phillips for an eye-watering £21 million and then breaking their club record by paying £24.4 million for Ghanaian midfielder Michael Essien.

The club record was also broken at Newcastle United, who beat Liverpool to the signing of striker Michael Owen, paying £17 million to Real Madrid for the England striker's services.

"Alan [Shearer] was a great help throughout and was instrumental in my decision. He even offered to give up his number nine shirt, but I've declined."

Michael Owen[1]

The season begins on 13 August and the champions Chelsea hit the ground running, winning their first nine games, conceding just three goals and building up a commanding lead at the top of the table. But when Arsenal manager Arsène Wenger questions the quality of the Chelsea side, it's leads to a stinging rebuke from José Mourinho.

"Wenger has a real problem with us and I think he is what you call in England a voyeur. He is someone who likes to watch other people. There are some guys who, when they are at home, have a big telescope to see what happens in other families. Wenger must be one of them – it is a sickness. He speaks, speaks, speaks about Chelsea."

José Mourinho retaliates with a classic quote[2]

"He's out of order, disconnected with reality and disrespectful. When you give success to stupid people, it makes them more stupid sometimes and not more intelligent."

Arsène Wenger, who clearly didn't take too kindly to the 'voyeur' comments.[3]

But José hadn't finished…

"At Stamford Bridge, we have a file of quotes from Mr. Wenger about Chelsea Football Club in the last 12 months – it is not a file of five pages. It is a file of 120 pages."

José Mourinho[4]

There's comedy gold at Highbury in late October when an attempt by Arsenal's Thierry Henry and Robert Pires to recreate Johan Cruyff's famous penalty for Ajax in 1982 ends in spectacular failure. The Gunners win a spot-kick against Manchester City and Pires puts the ball on the spot. But rather than go for goal, the French winger decides to knock the ball to his side, the idea being that his teammate Thierry Henry would run in and finish it off.

But it doesn't quite go to plan. As Pires shapes to tap it, he succeeds only in brushing the top of the ball with his studs, barely moving it off the penalty spot, and giving City's players ample opportunity to run in and clear.

"I take all the blame, it was my idea. If it had worked it would have been a brilliant idea, but it did not work."

Thierry Henry[5]

> **"We were within our rights, our intention was never to disrespect anyone. ... It didn't work for us, it was a shame but we still won the game. We didn't insult or hurt anyone."**
>
> Robert Pires[6]

With 10 wins from their first 11 league games, undefeated Chelsea are finally brought down to earth at Old Trafford in November where, on the 19th anniversary of Alex Ferguson's appointment as manager, Manchester United inflict the first defeat on the Blues, winning 1-0.

That said, it would be another 10 league games before Chelsea even so much as a drew another match.

> **"It was an important goal because it was against Chelsea, a huge rival, and stopped their 40-game unbeaten run. It gave us a massive three points at a time when there was a little bit of doom and gloom about the place."**
>
> Darren Fletcher, United goalscorer[7]

The United defeat would prove to be of little consequence as Chelsea steamrollered all before them. Indeed, the next time they lost in the league was at Middlesbrough on 11 February. Their dominance was such that José Mourinho seemed more concerned with the avian flu epidemic sweeping the planet than the pressure of being the Premier League frontrunners.

> **"For me, pressure is bird flu. It's not fun and I'm more scared of it than football."**
>
> José Mourinho[8]

There was no such progress on the Hampshire coast, though, where, just days after resigning from rivals Southampton, Harry Redknapp returns as manager of Portsmouth – his "spiritual home" – with the club threatened by relegation.

"No, why should it [relegation] worry me ... What difference is it going to make to my life in the long term? You think in 20 years' time I'm going to be sitting in some old nursing home somewhere worrying about what someone's saying? I've done my best ... No one's trying harder than I am to keep this club up now. So, if it doesn't work, what can I do? I can't kill myself over it."

Harry Redknapp, brutally honest as ever.[9]

Meanwhile, the intense rivalry between Manchester United and Liverpool hits new heights at the turn of the year as United beat Liverpool at Old Trafford and Gary Neville runs the length of the pitch to celebrate Rio Ferdinand's injury-time winner.

The trouble is that he does it right in front of the Liverpool fans...

> **"What are you meant to do? Smile sweetly and jog back to the halfway line? ... Increasingly people seem to want their footballers to be whiter than white and there are calls for sanctions over every little incident. Do they want a game of robots?"**
>
> Gary Neville explains his actions in *The Times*. He was charged with improper conduct and fined £5000.[10]

"I think there is a line and Neville crossed it. I've heard people say it's justified because he gets a lot of stick from our fans but the truth is he gets stick as he's been doing that for years."

And Liverpool's Jamie Carragher responds...[11]

On 14 January 2006, Thierry Henry equals Cliff Bastin's record of 150 league goals for Arsenal with a hat trick in a 7-0 thrashing of Middlesbrough.

> **"I knew I wasn't far away from Cliff Bastin's League goals record but I didn't step on the pitch thinking I wanted to beat Bastin's record. I just wanted to help the team..."**
>
> Thierry Henry on his latest record-breaking achievement.[12]

"This has been my toughest day as Middlesbrough manager without a shadow of a doubt. Down to 10 men with six teenagers on the park it was always going to be difficult. I've told the kids they're going to be good players in the future."

It wasn't such a happy day for Boro manager Steve McClaren.[13]

Later that week, Arsenal complete the signing of Southampton's 16-year-old star Theo Walcott. The fee, an initial £5 million rising to a possible £12.5 million, make him the most expensive 16-year-old in British football history.

> **"We are bitterly disappointed. The purpose of developing the best Academy in the country is not to sell scholars to larger clubs. We have done everything to keep Theo at Southampton. But his family and advisors are determined that he leave this club and go to Arsenal."**
>
> Rupert Lowe, Southampton's chairman[14]

"The kid can run through puddles and not make a splash. He's lightning."

Harry Redknapp, the manager who gave Walcott his debut at Southampton.[15]

But while Arsène Wenger was delighted with his new signing, he was getting increasingly riled by Chelsea's transparent pursuit of his England full-back Ashley Cole.

> *"If people come to your window and talk to your wife every night, you can't accept it without asking what's happening."*
>
> Arsène Wenger[16]

Meanwhile, Ashley Cole was aghast at the offer Arsenal had tabled in a bid to keep him at the club.

"When I heard Jonathan [Barnett, Cole's agent] repeat the figure of £55k, I nearly swerved off the road. I was so incensed. I was trembling with anger. I couldn't believe what I'd heard. I suppose it all started to fall apart for me from then on."

Ashley Cole, or 'Cashley' Cole as he was soon to be known by Gooners.[17]

At Newcastle United, striker Alan Shearer is forced to retire, his farewell season cut short by torn knee ligaments sustained in the 4-1 derby win over local rivals Sunderland, a game in which, naturally, he scored. He leaves the game as the Premier League's highest scorer, with 260 goals in 441 games.

"When I was a young boy I wanted to play for Newcastle United, I wanted to wear the number nine shirt and I wanted to score goals at St James' Park. I've lived my dream and I realise how lucky I've been to have done that."

Alan Shearer[18]

....

Chelsea's march to back-to-back titles, meanwhile, was irrepressible and the Blues sealed their second Premier League win with a comfortable 3-0 victory over Manchester United at Stamford Bridge. They even had two games to spare and equalled their own record of 29 league wins during the season.

José Mourinho, meanwhile, celebrates by throwing his winners' medal into the crowd.

"The medal was for everybody but I think the person in the crowd who got the medal is a lucky guy who goes home with a fantastic memory or goes to eBay and makes a fortune."

José Mourinho was nearly right. The medal was sold at auction by Bonhams for £21,600 in 2008.[19]

....

With Chelsea the runaway champions, there were still several issues to be decided. At the very foot of the table are Sunderland, who have won just three games all season to finish on a mere 15 points. It's the lowest ever total in the history of the Premier League. They are joined by Birmingham City and West Bromwich Albion.

The real relegation story, however, is at Portsmouth. Eight points adrift of safety, they win six of their last nine matches under Harry Redknapp.

"I think from January, when we got new players in, the place took a lift. It took a bit of time to get it up and running and then suddenly it turns."

Harry Redknapp, Pompey manager[20]

There's everything to play for in north London on the final day too as Arsenal, at home to Wigan in the final game at Highbury, and Spurs, away at West Ham, battle it out for fourth place and the final Champions League berth.

Yet Spurs, who only needed to match Arsenal's result to take fourth place, had to settle for fifth, their quest for Champions League football undone by a mysterious case of food poisoning before their final game against the Hammers, a match they lost 2-1.

"The club tried to get the match called off, but in vain, so we just had to play through it feeling like death ... Once the game started players were literally running off the pitch. It was carnage."

Tottenham's Jermaine Jenas on the mystery of 'lasagnegate'.[21]

Fourth place instead goes to Arsenal who, resplendent in a redcurrant kit similar to that worn by the team when they first moved to Highbury in 1913, ran out 4-2 winners, courtesy of a hat trick from Golden Boot winner Thierry Henry. It's also the final Arsenal game for club legend Dennis Bergkamp.

But their season ends in despair as they lose the Champions League final to Barcelona in Paris. The Gunners take the lead through Sol Campbell but also have goalkeeper Jens Lehmann sent off and concede two late goals to miss out.

"Nobody will ever forget him."

Arsenal manager Arsène Wenger on Dennis Bergkamp[22]

"I kissed the ground goodbye ... Highbury is just a special place."

Thierry Henry[23]

Games Played: 38

Pos	Team	GD	Pts
1	Chelsea	+50	91
2	Manchester United	+38	83
3	Liverpool	+32	82
4	Arsenal	+37	67
5	Tottenham Hotspur	+15	65
6	Blackburn Rovers	+9	63
7	Newcastle United	+5	58
8	Bolton Wanderers	+8	56
9	West Ham United	-3	55
10	Wigan Athletic	-7	51
11	Everton	-15	50
12	Fulham	-10	48
13	Charlton Athletic	-14	47
14	Middlesbrough	-10	45
15	Manchester City	-5	43
16	Aston Villa	-13	42
17	Portsmouth	-25	38
18	Birmingham City	-22	34
19	West Bromwich Albion	-27	30
20	Sunderland	-43	15

CHAMPIONS: Chelsea

RUNNERS-UP: Manchester United

RELEGATED: Birmingham City, West Bromwich Albion, Sunderland

PROMOTED: Reading, Sheffield United, Watford

TOP GOALSCORER: Thierry Henry, Arsenal – 27

PLAYER OF THE SEASON: Steven Gerrard, Liverpool

MANAGER OF THE SEASON: José Mourinho, Chelsea

DID YOU KNOW? *With 27 goals, Arsenal's Thierry Henry actually outscored the entire Sunderland team for this season.*

PREMIER LEAGUE 2006/07

Homecomings and Farewells

After the emotional scenes at Highbury at the end of the previous season, it was time for Arsenal to unveil their new home, the £390 million, 60,000-capacity Emirates Stadium.

The first game at the ground is a testimonial for Dennis Bergkamp against his old club, Ajax, on 22 July 2006.

"It's difficult to say goodbye. I've had a fantastic time over the last 11 years and a big part were the fans and how they treated me – they have been fantastic."

Arsenal legend Dennis Bergkamp[1]

Not to be undone, Manchester United also revealed the new look Old Trafford with extensive renovations taking their capacity to 76,000 and making the Theatre of Dreams the largest club stadium in the United Kingdom.

Increasingly, the nation's football clubs found themselves the subject of foreign takeovers. Aston Villa, for example, was bought by the American entrepreneur Randy Lerner, while in February 2007 the Liverpool chairman announced that he had accepted a £219 million takeover bid from American businessmen George Gillett and Tom Hicks.

On the pitch, meanwhile, it was West Ham that landed the biggest transfer coup of the close season, capturing the services of Argentinian World Cup duo Carlos Tevez and Javier Mascherano in a deal shrouded in secrecy.

"West Ham United are delighted to announce the double signing of Argentinian World Cup stars Carlos Tevez and Javier Mascherano from Brazilian club Corinthians. The pair have been signed for an undisclosed fee and put pen-to-paper on permanent contracts with the club this afternoon. All other aspects of the transfers will remain confidential and undisclosed."

West Ham club statement[2]

And after two titles in successive seasons, Chelsea's pursuit of a hat trick of Premier League wins was boosted by the arrival of prolific AC Milan striker and former European Footballer of the Year Andriy Shevchenko and the German international Michael Ballack for the season ahead.

"Today is a day when the dream became reality. Andriy has always been my first choice for Chelsea since I arrived ... He is a champion and he is joining a team of champions."

José Mourinho, Chelsea manager[3]

Controversially, Chelsea also sign Arsenal's Ashley Cole (with William Gallas going the other way). The England full-back had been holding out for more money from the Gunners but had, famously, been taken aback by the amount they were offering – just £55,000 per week.

The season begins on 19 August and Manchester United signal their intentions right from the off, rattling in four goals in the first 19 minutes against Fulham before running out 5-1 winners.

"I couldn't be any more pleased ... We know the target we must aim for this season and it's a target that means we must hit the ground running and keep it that way."

Sir Alex Ferguson, Manchester United manager[4]

After five games, however, there was a surprise leader of the Premier League as Portsmouth took 13 points from a possible 15 to lead the pack.

"We have been brilliant so far this season. We are trying to finish above our highest previous finish in the Premiership which is 13th. We've had a good start but we're not getting carried away."

Harry Redknapp, Portsmouth manager. His side would better 13th too, finishing ninth.[5]

But it's not all good news for Pompey. At Manchester City's Eastlands Stadium, City defender Ben Thatcher knocks out Portsmouth's Pedro Mendes, deliberately leading with his elbow as the two challenge for the ball. It's a vicious, violent assault and while the Pompey defender is hospitalised, Thatcher later receives an eight-match ban and is fined six weeks' wages by his club.

"The moment was terrible. After the incident, I do not remember anything after that until I was in hospital. It is the worst thing that has ever happened to me in my career."

Pedro Mendes[6]

"What happened on Wednesday was indefensible ... But I can assure everybody, this has hit the player very hard. There is no bravado about him. He has gone home, turned on the TV and seen the challenge. The more you watch it, the worse it gets."

Stuart Pearce, Manchester City manager[7]

With only one win from their first four games (including a comprehensive 3-0 defeat in the Merseyside derby against Everton), Liverpool's stuttering start to the campaign was brightened up by a spectacular goal by their Spanish midfielder Xabi Alonso as the Reds hosted Newcastle. Spotting the visitors' keeper Steve Harper off his line, Alonso took a shot from over 60 yards, deep inside his own half, and watched as it sailed over Harper and into the net.

"I was thinking of telling him off when he didn't pass to Steven Gerrard who had made a good run forward. I was really disappointed in him but then, afterwards, I had to say congratulations."

Rafa Benitez, Liverpool manager[8]

Back at Eastlands and there is more trouble for Manchester City to deal with as their midfielder Joey Barton drops his shorts and bares his bottom to the visiting Everton fans at the end of their 1-1 draw.

"I didn't see it. But I see it [the Barton bottom] every week. Not in the Biblical sense, obviously."

Stuart Pearce, Manchester City manager[9]

"It was a bit cheeky wasn't it? But I don't think it was that bad. It would have been worse if he'd turned round and dropped the front of his shorts instead. I don't think there's anything wrong with a couple of butt cheeks personally ... If anybody's offended by seeing a backside, get real. Maybe they're just jealous that he's got a real nice tight one, with no cellulite or anything."

Plymouth manager Ian Holloway has his say on the matter. Barton was later fined £2000.[10]

On Saturday 14 October, during a game against Reading, Chelsea goalkeeper Petr Cech sustains a fractured skull as he collides with Stephen Hunt's knee. He is out of the game for over three months and, to this day, he has worn a head guard during games ever since.

"Things could have been different. The doctors tried not to scare me too much and I never asked too much. But if you ask my wife, even now, she does not look too well. For her, the experience was a thousand times worse than it was for me. It was a very close call."

Petr Cech recalls his injury 10 years on.[11]

December saw two key goals in the Premier League with West Ham's Teddy Sheringham becoming the event's oldest ever scorer, aged 40 years and 268 days, and, on 30 December, Fulham's Moritz Volz scoring the 15,000th goal in the history of the competition, as he bagged the opening goal in a 2-2 draw in the West London derby against Chelsea. Not that he realised...

> **"I only realised when I came in after the game and everyone wanted to speak to me – and that didn't normally happen."**
>
> Moritz '15,000' Volz, complete with new nickname.[12]

It's February and as the FA Premier League renamed itself as the 'Premier League' (adding a new logo and typeface), Manchester United continued their irrepressible surge towards regaining the title. They win all their matches in the month and then follow it up by taking maximum points in March too to open up a commanding nine-point lead.

Meanwhile, on 17 March, at White Hart Lane, Spurs' goalkeeper Paul Robinson gets on the scoresheet in the 3-1 win over Watford, his 83-yard free kick bouncing over the head of his England colleague Ben Foster.

> **"It's a freak goal … I didn't celebrate the goal out of the respect that I have for any goalkeeper. It was fantastic to score a goal, but I can't really pretend that I meant it."**
>
> Tottenham's Paul Robinson[13]

"It's not been a great day in the office for me."

Ben Foster, Watford keeper[14]

On 31 March, a day when a new Premier League attendance record was set as 76,098 fans packed into Old Trafford to see United play Blackburn, top four contenders Liverpool and Arsenal faced up at Anfield with Rafa Benitez's side emerging as 4-1 winners, thanks to a perfect hat trick – left foot, right foot and header – from striker Peter Crouch, a player linked with a move away from the club.

> **"I want to remain part of the manager's plans but he keeps his cards close to his chest. I am as happy as I have ever been and determined to prove I am worth my place. No one is safe at a big club like this."**
>
> Peter Crouch[15]

> *"He was superb. Everything he did was intelligent. He has the size of a basketball player but the skill of a real football player."*

Arsène Wenger, Arsenal manager[16]

But while their title aspirations are over, Liverpool still progress to another Champions League final, losing to the team they defeated two years earlier in Istanbul, AC Milan. The only challengers to United's supremacy are reigning champions Chelsea who, having taken the League Cup (beating United in the final), win nine league matches in a row to close the gap on Alex Ferguson's leaders.

While Chelsea's run at the top of the table catches the eye, so too does the run that West Ham put together at the foot of it. Ten points from safety on 4 March, they win seven of their last nine games to beat the drop, with Carlos Tevez bagging seven goals in the process, including the winner at Old Trafford on the final day of the season.

> **"They couldn't have come to Old Trafford on a better day ... the edge was off our game. Nonetheless we still had 25 shots on goal. I think we did our best and I don't think people can criticise us. I feel for Neil Warnock and Sheffield United but, when he sees the statistics, he will know we were very unlucky to lose."**

Sir Alex Ferguson, Manchester United manager[17]

Their survival sends Sheffield United down but it doesn't end there, as questions over the legitimacy of Tevez's registration eventually see the matter go to court. Though West Ham are fined £5.5 million for breaking Premier League rules, they are spared a points deduction – and it's a decision that sees Sheffield United take legal action to have the ruling overturned.

> "We've had a lot of people criticise us for taking it this far – but that's what justice is all about. But this still doesn't make it right for me or the United fans – or anyone else involved ... If it had been a big club, the truth would have come out earlier and it would have been sorted."

Neil Warnock, Sheffield United manager. The matter would eventually be settled out of court in March 2009, with West Ham agreeing to pay Sheffield United compensation.[18]

That result didn't affect the destination of the title as Chelsea's 1-1 draw with Arsenal in their penultimate game had handed the title to Manchester United. It is the Red Devils' ninth title in 15 years and all in Alex Ferguson's 20th year in charge at the club.

"The Premier League is such a competitive league and the focus and the pressure on the big clubs makes it a focus for us. I used to have an obsession of winning in Europe but the Premiership has become a priority..."

Sir Alex Ferguson, a winner yet again.[19]

Games Played: 38

Pos	Team	GD	Pts
1	Manchester United	+56	89
2	Chelsea	+40	83
3	Liverpool	+30	68
4	Arsenal	+28	68
5	Tottenham Hotspur	+3	60
6	Everton	+16	58
7	Bolton Wanderers	-5	56
8	Reading	+5	55
9	Portsmouth	+3	54
10	Blackburn Rovers	-2	52
11	Aston Villa	+2	50
12	Middlesbrough	-5	46
13	Newcastle United	-9	43
14	Manchester City	-15	42
15	West Ham United	-24	41
16	Fulham	-22	39
17	Wigan Athletic	-22	38
18	Sheffield United	-23	38
19	Charlton Athletic	-26	34
20	Watford	-30	28

CHAMPIONS: Manchester United

RUNNERS-UP: Chelsea

RELEGATED: Sheffield United, Charlton Athletic, Watford

PROMOTED: Sunderland, Birmingham City, Derby County

TOP GOALSCORER: Didier Drogba, Chelsea – 20

PLAYER OF THE SEASON: Cristiano Ronaldo, Manchester United

MANAGER OF THE SEASON: Sir Alex Ferguson, Manchester United

DID YOU KNOW? *Sheffield United scored just eight goals away from home this season, equalling the record for the lowest total ever.*

PREMIER LEAGUE 2007/08

World Class

This was the season where the English Premier League announced that from now on, their flagship competition would no longer be called the Barclays Premiership and would, instead, now be known as the 'Barclays Premier League'. It was a subtle change – so subtle, in fact, that to this day, fans, players and managers still invariably call it the Premiership.

Change was also afoot among the Premiership's – sorry, Premier League's – clubs as Newcastle United were taken over by the Sports Direct billionaire Mike Ashley and Manchester City swapped Stuart Pearce for former England manager Sven-Goran Eriksson.

There were some high-profile transfers in the summer window as well. Liverpool signed the prolific Atletico Madrid striker Fernando Torres for £20 million, while rivals Manchester United headed to Portugal to snap up Nani and Anderson from Sporting and Porto respectively. The Red Devils also secured the services of Argentinian free agent Carlos Tevez.

But as an influx of foreign talent flooded into the English game, there was one notable departure as Arsenal's Thierry Henry, the club's all-time highest scorer, joined Barcelona. He was replaced by the Brazilian striker Eduardo.

"I never considered leaving Arsenal. But I was 29 years old and in form, I thought all the guys left and I did not know if Arsène [Wenger] would be staying. It was not easy and when I left I cried. I'm not ashamed to say it. I'm a competitor and I had to leave."

Thierry Henry[1]

The season begins on 11 August...

> *"It is omelettes and eggs. No eggs – no omelettes! It depends on the quality of the eggs. In the supermarket ... some are more expensive than others and some give you better omelettes. So when the class one eggs are in Waitrose and you cannot go there, you have a problem."*
>
> After just three wins in their first seven games, Chelsea boss questions the quality of his squad.[2]

Manchester United's indifferent start to the season – they drew their first two games and lost the third to Manchester City – was compounded by the red card their star player, Cristiano Ronaldo, received for headbutting Portsmouth's Richard Hughes.

> **"Cristiano has fallen into the trap of [provocation], which has happened to him a few times. He has only himself to blame and it left us with 10 men ... You have to remind yourself that you are a better player than these players and that is why they are doing it."**
>
> Wise words from Ronaldo's manager, Sir Alex Ferguson.[3]

Five games into the season and newly promoted Derby County are bottom of the table with just one point to show for their efforts. After a 6-0 drubbing at Liverpool, one bookmaker even begins paying out on the team to be relegated, despite there being 33 games still to play.

> **"We are still not competing in the manner we should and we won't pick up points until we start doing so."**
>
> Billy Davies, Derby County manager[4]

On paper, Portsmouth versus Reading might not have looked like the most appetising fixture on the Premier League schedule, but when the two teams met on 29 September it turned out to be the highest scoring match in Premier League history, with Pompey winning 7-4. What made the game even more remarkable was that all 11 goals were scored by different players.

> "It's difficult to analyse a match like that and if
> you try you will be there a very long time ... We
> played a full part in the game – I don't think many
> teams will come here this season and score four."

A perplexed Steve Coppell, Reading manager.[5]

Having steered Chelsea to six trophies in three years, including back-to-back
Premier League titles, and remained unbeaten at Stamford Bridge in the league,
José Mourinho parts company with Chelsea. The Blues have made an indifferent
start to the Premier League campaign but the final straw comes after a disappointing
1-1 draw in the Champions League with Norwegian side Rosenborg.

**"José did not resign and he was not sacked. What is clear,
though, is we had all reached a point where the relationship
between the club and José had broken down. This was despite
genuine attempts over several months by all parties to resolve
certain differences."**

Chelsea FC statement[6]

> *"I would love to gather all the fans together to say goodbye
> but they would crush me with their love."*

José Mourinho makes his own farewells.[7]

**"Nothing surprises me in football, but if I said I was astounded
that would be an understatement."**

Ray Wilkins on José Mourinho's departure from Chelsea. He would be appointed
Chelsea's first-team coach.[8]

> **"Chelsea looked forward. I look forward. They move
> on. I move on."**

José Mourinho, before he took his new team, Inter Milan, to Chelsea for a
Champions League last-16 tie in 2010.[9]

Soon after, Chelsea hired a new coach – and it was an appointment that had
most in the game scratching their heads. Step forward 52-year-old Avram
Grant, former Israeli national coach, close personal friend of owner Roman
Abramovich and, since July 2007, Chelsea's Director of Football.

"I am not 'the Special One'. I'm the normal one. But my wife says I am special. What am I like? I am 180cm."

New manager Avram Grant[10]

"Avram Grant is going to be as welcome as Camilla at Diana's memorial. This guy is not well-loved at Chelsea. He is not going to last."

Pat Nevin, former Chelsea player and BBC pundit[11]

"If we're talking lookalikes, he's Toad of Toad Hall, isn't he?"

Ian Holloway on Chelsea boss Avram Grant.[12]

Grant's first game in charge is at Old Trafford. Ten-man Chelsea lose 2-0 and the new gaffer isn't happy with the result or with the referee, Mike Dean.

"The referee made three mistakes only. The red card, playing too much time at the end of the first half [when Man Utd scored] and the penalty. Apart from that he was good."

Avram Grant, Chelsea manager[13]

At the end of October, Tottenham Hotspur dispense with the services of manager Martin Jol and, despite a clamour for José Mourinho to be given the job, they eventually replace him with the highly rated Sevilla coach Juande Ramos, whom they had been courting for some time.

"Martin Jol was literally a dead man walking at Spurs."

BBC pundit Steve Claridge, on the money as ever.[14]

November saw the game of the season as Arsenal hosted Manchester United, with both teams level on points and goal difference. In a breathtaking match, Arsenal twice came from behind to snatch a 2-2 draw, with William Gallas, who had also scored an own goal, securing a point with an injury-time equaliser.

> **"Arsenal are my favourite team right now and I think they are the best performing team in the Premier League."**
>
> Brazilian legend Pelé gives his verdict on Arsenal's title challenge.[15]

Derby County, meanwhile, decide to look for a new manager, letting Billy Davies go on the same day that he's due to collect the Coach of the Year Award at the BBC East Midlands Sports Awards.

> **"The team is not good enough for the Premier League. That's no reflection or disrespect to the players. They know that. They're not good enough."**
>
> One of Billy Davies' parting shots as Derby manager.[16]

Two days later they appoint Paul Jewell as their new manager.

> **"I've got more points on my driving licence."**
>
> Paul Jewell reflects on Derby's perilous position.[17]

As the year draws to a close, there's a Premier League first at the JJB Stadium where both Wigan's Marcus Bent and Blackburn's Roque Santa Cruz score hat tricks in the home side's 5-3 win. It's the first time that two players on opposing teams had scored hat tricks during the same game.

Meanwhile, Ryan Giggs had been given the captain's armband at Manchester United, as the Red Devils try to keep pace with Arsenal at the top of the table.

> **"Gary Neville is the club captain but has been injured for the best part of a year now – and Giggsy's taken on the mantelpiece."**
>
> Rio Ferdinand, Neville's teammate[18]

There are changes afoot in mid-table, too. On 9 January, with the club lying in 11th place in the Premier League, Newcastle United and manager Sam Allardyce go their separate ways. He has had just 24 games in charge. While disappointing results were cited as a reason, it was clear that Allardyce felt hamstrung by the club's management structure.

"The only decisions I'm making at the moment are whether I have tea, coffee, toast or cornflakes in the morning."

Sam Allardyce[19]

> "I am sure we will see pictures of Sam in his Speedos walking along a beach somewhere. That won't be a pretty sight."
>
> Wigan boss Steve Bruce speculates on what Sam Allardyce will do next.[20]

Within a week of Allardyce's departure, Newcastle had hired a new manager, welcoming back fans' favourite Kevin Keegan for a second spell at the club, 12 years after narrowly missing out on the Premier League title. But not before the Magpies, with first-team coach Steve Kean in temporary charge, had been hammered 6-0 by Manchester United, a game in which Ronaldo scored his one and only hat trick for the Red Devils. It's a performance that draws all manner of praise.

"The one thing Cristiano Ronaldo has is pace, quick feet and a great eye for goal."

BBC summariser Chris Waddle[21]

"He's six-foot something, fit as a flea, good-looking – he's got to have something wrong with him. Hopefully he's hung like a hamster! That would make us all feel better!"

Ian Holloway gives his own unique take on CR7[22]

On 23 February, Birmingham City host Arsenal at St Andrews and while the game ends in an entertaining 2-2 draw, it's overshadowed by a serious injury to Arsenal's Eduardo, who suffers a broken left fibula and an open dislocation of his left ankle after a straight red-card challenge by Birmingham's Martin Taylor.

"This guy should never play again. The answer is 'he is usually not that type of guy'. It's like a guy who kills one time in his life – it's enough, you have a dead person. It is absolutely horrendous..."

Arsène Wenger vents his frustration at the Taylor tackle.[23]

It's also a month where the Premier League broaches the idea of a 39th game, wherein one additional game would be added to the fixture list and played abroad in one of the competition's new markets. It's a novel idea but it's met with resistance from clubs, administrators and supporters.

"A nonsense idea."

UEFA's response to the Premier League's proposal.[24]

With three matches left to play, it had seemed as though Fulham's stay in the Premier League was all but over. Five points adrift of safety, Roy Hodgson's team were 2-0 down at Manchester City with 20 minutes to play before they staged a remarkable comeback and sealed an astonishing win in injury time, thanks to a Diomansy Kamara goal. They then beat Birmingham City at home before a narrow 1-0 victory over Portsmouth on the final day somehow maintained their top-flight status.

"In all the jubilation, I must say we were not that far away from it being us and not them. But it feels great!"

Roy Hodgson, Fulham manager, on the greatest of escapes.[25]

"In hindsight, all we can do really is congratulate Fulham. I guess they have put a real dampener on our day."

Reading boss Steve Coppell, whose side were relegated alongside Birmingham City and Derby County.[26]

If anybody had thought that a team couldn't perform worse than Sunderland's meagre total of 15 points in 2005/6, they were wrong. Derby County had ended the season bottom of the table with just 11 points. They had won just one game, drawn eight and lost 29. They had conceded 89 goals and scored only 20 and were an unfathomable 25 points adrift of safety.

The race for the title, however, goes into the final day. Arsenal's poor form in the run-in – they could only muster one win in eight games from late-February to mid-April – saw a straight shoot-out between leaders Manchester United and defending champions Chelsea. After their indifferent start to the campaign, the Blues had got back on track, losing just once since a 2-0 defeat at Old Trafford on 23 September. Now, they needed to win at home to Bolton and hope that United failed to beat Wigan, as the Red Devils enjoyed a vastly superior goal difference.

It wasn't to be. United wrapped up a comfortable 2-0 victory while Chelsea laboured to a 1-1 draw with Bolton. United had their 17th league title, just one behind Liverpool's all-time record.

Much of the credit for United's success would go to the relentless brilliance of their Portuguese winger, Cristiano Ronaldo. The undisputed Player of the Season, he had scored 31 goals in 34 league games (at a rate of one every 88.6 minutes) and a total of 42 across all competitions. He had won the Champions League and he would also go on to claim the first of four Ballons d'Or.

> **"I had played with some great players in Roy Keane, Ryan Giggs, Paul Scholes, David Beckham, Eric Cantona and Mark Hughes. Because of their longevity at the club, they may be ranked above Ronaldo as United greats. But no one was as good as Ronaldo in that two-year period."**
>
> High praise indeed from Ronaldo's Manchester United teammate Gary Neville.[27]

It wouldn't be the only time United edge out Chelsea. The two sides meet in the Champions League final in Moscow and a tense match is decided on penalties. United, thanks to John Terry's slip and miss from the spot and Nicolas Anelka's failure to convert his penalty, take the trophy once more. It's yet another trophy in the Old Trafford cabinet and a hammer blow for Chelsea and their skipper.

> *"I still have a few times a year when I wake up and, bang, it's on my mind. It'll never go. It's one of those things."*
>
> Chelsea's John Terry, still hurting in 2015.[28]

Games Played: 38

Pos	Team	GD	Pts
1	Manchester United	+58	87
2	Chelsea	+39	85
3	Arsenal	+43	83
4	Liverpool	+39	76
5	Everton	+22	65
6	Aston Villa	+20	60
7	Blackburn Rovers	+2	58
8	Portsmouth	+8	57
9	Manchester City	-8	55
10	West Ham United	-8	49
11	Tottenham Hotspur	+5	46
12	Newcastle United	-20	43
13	Middlesbrough	-10	42
14	Wigan Athletic	-17	40
15	Sunderland	-23	39
16	Bolton Wanderers	-18	37
17	Fulham	-22	36
18	Reading	-25	36
19	Birmingham City	-16	35
20	Derby County	-69	11

CHAMPIONS: Manchester United

RUNNERS-UP: Chelsea

RELEGATED: Reading, Birmingham City, Derby County

PROMOTED: Stoke City, Hull City, West Bromwich Albion

TOP GOALSCORER: Cristiano Ronaldo, Manchester United – 31

PLAYER OF THE SEASON: Cristiano Ronaldo, Manchester United

MANAGER OF THE SEASON: Sir Alex Ferguson, Manchester United

DID YOU KNOW? *Derby County's record low points total saw them become the first team to be relegated from the Premier League in March.*

PREMIER LEAGUE 2008/09

Back-to-back Brilliance

With back-to-back titles and the Champions League trophy already under their belt, Manchester United's dominance showed no sign of diminishing. During the course of the 2008/9 season they would also become the first English club to win the FIFA Club World Cup, beating LDQ Quito in Yokohama, Japan.

With their Premier League rivals desperate to keep pace with United, there was change afoot at Stamford Bridge where, after the sacking of Avram Grant in May, the Blues turned to Luiz Felipe Scolari, coach of Brazil's 2002 World Cup winning team, as their new manager. The 60-year-old was hired on an eye-watering salary of £6.25 million, making him the highest-paid manager in the world.

"Felipe has great qualities. He is one of the world's top coaches with a record of success at country and club level. He gets the best out of a talented squad of players and his ambitions and expectations match ours. He was the outstanding choice."

Chelsea FC statement[1]

"If someone talks about my private life, for example, I'll give them a good punching. I'm not interested in suing. I like to sort things out my way."

Luiz Felipe Scolari on his interpersonal skills.[2]

Dugouts got a little bit cosier, too, as now teams were allowed seven substitutes rather than five in their match-day squad. The season starts on Saturday 16 August.

Two weeks later, Manchester City, so long the poor relation in the city's football rivalry, were bought by Sheikh Mansour's Abu Dhabi United Group. With new – and very rich – owners, City had become genuine title contenders almost overnight.

> *"We are not going to do crazy stuff, but it makes sense for us to build a dynasty ... I think we are going to have a blast doing it!"*
>
> Khaldoon Al Mubarak, Manchester City's new chairman[3]

Almost immediately, and just moments before the summer transfer window closed, City signed Real Madrid's Brazilian wunderkind Robinho for a new British record £32.5 million. So much for no 'crazy stuff'.

"I have said that in order to compete with the best teams in the Premier League we have to be in the market for players of this calibre, and Robinho is undoubtedly one of the best players in the world."

Manchester City's new manager Mark Hughes. The Welshman was appointed in June 2008 following Sven-Goran Eriksson's sacking.[4]

Not to be outdone, rivals Manchester United strike a deadline day deal of their own, landing Tottenham's Dimitar Berbatov for £30.75 million, despite interest from City.

Within days of the transfer window closing, Kevin Keegan calls time on his second spell in charge at Newcastle, citing a breakdown in relations with the club's board for his departure.

"I've been working desperately hard to find a way forward with the directors, but sadly that has not proved possible. It's my opinion that a manager must have the right to manage and that clubs should not impose upon any manager any player that he does not want."

Kevin Keegan's statement[5]

Out of the blue, he was replaced by one-time Wimbledon boss Joe Kinnear, a shock move that was met with incredulity from the club's passionate following.

> **"The fans will be disappointed [with the appointment], I understand that, but I can't do anything about it."**
>
> Joe Kinnear, the new – and largely unwanted – Newcastle United manager.[6]

Four days into his tenure, Kinnear snapped during his first press conference as manager, launching an expletive-heavy tirade at journalists, with one, the *Daily Mirror's* Simon Bird, in the firing line for asking why he had given his under-performing team a day off on his very first day in charge.

> **"Which one is Simon Bird? You're a ****! ... It is none of your f****** business. What the f*** are you going to do? You ain't got the balls to be a f****** manager. F****** day off. Do I want your opinion? Do I have to listen to you?"**
>
> Joe Kinnear [7]

On the pitch, it was Chelsea that made the early pace. Buoyed by the signing of the Portuguese playmaker Deco, they took 20 points from their opening eight matches to stand level with Liverpool and the surprise package of the division, newly promoted Hull City. The Tigers had won six of their first nine games in the highest league, a run that had included away wins at both Arsenal and Spurs.

> *"It's expectancy levels that I've got to manage. I don't mind everybody on a high and getting excited because it's their first season in the top flight, but we have to be realistic."*
>
> Phil Brown, Hull City manager[8]

With just two draws and six defeats from their first eight games and the team languishing in the relegation zone, Spurs sack manager Juande Ramos, replacing him with Portsmouth's Harry Redknapp. Come the end of the season he will have guided them to the comfort of eighth place and to the final of the League Cup.

"It's a big opportunity to manage a big club before I retire."

New Spurs boss Harry Redknapp[9]

October was also the month where Chelsea's 86-match record for the most home games undefeated in the Premier League came to an end, courtesy of Xabi Alonso's winner for high-flying Liverpool at Stamford Bridge.

> **"Their run couldn't go on forever, they had to lose sometime and I'm just glad it was to us. We're top of the league now but it's a long way to go. It's only one game."**
>
> Jamie Carragher, Liverpool defender[10]

Meanwhile, in north London there's an outrageous 40-yard volley from former Arsenal player David Bentley that helps Spurs rescue a 4-4 draw with the Gunners at the Emirates.

> **"Bentley ... Oh he's seen Almunia out of his goal! What a brilliant effort! David Bentley! Showing Arsenal what they let go!"**
>
> Martin Tyler, Sky Sports commentator[11]

> **"I'm so happy! I'm buzzin' ... I'm going to fly home tonight. I feel like Superman at the minute!"**
>
> Spurs hero David Bentley in his post-match television interview.[12]

As new England manager Fabio Capello continues to expound on the benefits of better diets for the national team's players, Spurs' boss Harry Redknapp remains unconvinced.

> *"If you can't pass the ball properly, a bowl of pasta's not going to make that much difference."*
>
> Harry Redknapp, Spurs' manager[13]

As Manchester United surge up the table, a 5-0 thrashing of Stoke City sparking a 16-match unbeaten run in the Premier League, there's renewed interest in their Portuguese superstar Ronaldo, chiefly from Real Madrid.

"Do you think I would enter into a contract with that mob? Absolutely no chance. I would not sell them a virus. That is a 'No' by the way. There is no agreement whatsoever between the clubs."

United manager Sir Alex Ferguson scotches rumours that Ronaldo is on his way.[14]

Following five defeats in six games and with Sunderland lying 18th in the table, Roy Keane resigns as manager of Sunderland at the beginning of December. The Irishman has been in charge for two and a half years.

Boxing Day 2008 would go down as the one and only time that a Premier League manager has conducted a halftime team talk on the pitch. It came at Manchester City's Eastlands stadium, where Hull City are four goals down by the break and Tigers' manager Phil Brown is less than impressed.

"Why not conduct a team talk on the pitch? Why not do it in front of everyone. It wasn't a knee-jerk reaction. It was definitely the right thing to do. If it meant bruising one or two egos so be it."

Phil Brown explains himself. His team went on to lose 5-1.[15]

"It might have been better doing it away from the pitch to be honest. Doing a team talk like that on the pitch means everyone can see you and it doesn't look too good."

Hull's Brazilian striker Geovanni wasn't quite so keen on the idea.[16]

The transfer window opens again and rumours are rife...

'KAKA'

As Manchester City prepared a world record £100 million bid for AC Milan's Kaka, 25-year-old City fan Chris Atkinson took to the ink and had the Brazilian superstar's name tattooed across his chest. Kaka stayed in Italy.[17]

In Liverpool, Reds' manager Rafa Benitez is determined not to be lured into Sir Alex Ferguson's famous mind games. But as he reels off 'fact' after 'fact' about the United manager, it's clear to everyone that he's failed miserably.

"But I want to talk about facts. I want to be clear, I do not want to play mind games too early, although they seem to want to start. But I have seen some facts..."

Don't go there, Rafa Benitez...[18]

"I think he was an angry man. He must have been disturbed for some reason. I think you have got to cut through the venom of it and hopefully he'll reflect and understand what he said was absolutely ridiculous."

And Fergie's reply...[19]

While United and their remarkable consistency seems to be getting under the skin of their rivals, it's also getting other managers the sack and after just seven months in the job, Chelsea bring an end to Luiz Felipe Scolari's reign as coach, citing the need "to maintain a challenge for trophies" as they sit seven points adrift of United. The Dutchman Guus Hiddink is appointed interim manager.

"I'm just very shocked by what's happened. He's a great man. Unfortunately we weren't playing well and it falls on his head. Maybe they should look at some of us. We did under-achieve."

John Terry, Chelsea captain[20]

At the other end of the table it's worrying times for the Toon Army as Newcastle United fight against relegation. It's a task made even more complicated by manager Joe Kinnear standing aside after heart surgery. With eight games to guarantee their survival, they turn to club legend Alan Shearer.

"My job is to keep Newcastle United in the Premier League ... I envisage watching Newcastle next year playing in the Premier League. It's a massive challenge, we've got injuries but we'll give it a right good go."

Alan Shearer at his first managerial press conference.[21]

Come the end of April and Liverpool were still on Manchester United's heels – they had even beaten United 4-1 at Old Trafford. But their progress was halted first by 17-year-old Federico Macheda's late winner for United over Aston Villa...

"Great turn by Machedaaaaaaa! Astonishing!"

Martin Tyler, Sky Sports commentator[22]

And then by their own 4-4 draw with Arsenal at Anfield, a match that saw the Gunners' Andrey Arshavin become the first player in 60 years to score four goals against Liverpool at Anfield.

> **"I have been in this job a long time and not many players get four goals in a top game like that."**
>
> Arsène Wenger, Arsenal manager[23]

Newcastle's 16-year stay in the top flight came to an end after a Damien Duff own goal against Aston Villa consigned them to the Championship. They were joined by Middlesbrough and already relegated West Bromwich Albion. Alan Shearer's eight games in charge had yielded just five points. To this day, he has never managed another club.

"It's a football club I love. You've seen what it means to our fans. I am hurting. I am raw inside. But the simple fact is that big mistakes have been made and we're now paying the price for that."

Alan Shearer[24]

At the other end of the table, Manchester United wrapped up their third straight Premier League title with a game to spare. Four points clear of Liverpool, seven clear of Chelsea and a massive 18 points ahead of Arsenal in fourth place, it had been a masterclass in front-running where experience, attacking flair and defensive consistency counted for everything.

And so what if they were outclassed by Barcelona in the Champions League final in Rome? It was still very much job done.

Games Played: 38

Pos	Team	GD	Pts
1	Manchester United	+44	90
2	Liverpool	+50	86
3	Chelsea	+44	83
4	Arsenal	+31	72
5	Everton	+18	63
6	Aston Villa	+6	62
7	Fulham	+5	53
8	Tottenham Hotspur	0	51
9	West Ham United	-3	51
10	Manchester City	+8	50
11	Wigan Athletic	-11	45
12	Stoke City	-17	45
13	Bolton Wanderers	-12	41
14	Portsmouth	-19	41
15	Blackburn Rovers	-20	41
16	Sunderland	-20	36
17	Hull City	-25	35
18	Newcastle United	-19	34
19	Middlesbrough	-29	32
20	West Bromwich Albion	-31	32

CHAMPIONS: Manchester United

RUNNERS-UP: Liverpool

RELEGATED: Newcastle United, Middlesbrough, West Bromwich Albion

PROMOTED: Birmingham City, Wolverhampton Wanderers, Burnley

TOP GOALSCORER: Nicolas Anelka, Chelsea – 19

PLAYER OF THE SEASON: Ryan Giggs, Manchester United

MANAGER OF THE SEASON: Sir Alex Ferguson, Manchester United

DID YOU KNOW? *Manchester United goalkeeper Edwin van der Sar equalled the Premier League record for the highest number of clean sheets this season, with 21 in total.*

PREMIER LEAGUE 2009/10

More Than Special

It had been something that Manchester United had been resisting for several seasons but the lure of Real Madrid had finally proved too much for Cristiano Ronaldo. The Portuguese superstar put pen to paper on a world record €94 million transfer with the Spanish giants in June, his five-year deal earning him €11 million a year and including a mind-boggling €1 billion buyout clause.

Although United would bring in Wigan's Antonio Valencia and former Liverpool and England striker Michael Owen, they would still have to seek an unprecedented fourth consecutive league title without their star player.

"For me, I have made my childhood dream a reality, which was nothing less than playing for Real Madrid."

Cristiano Ronaldo on the day he was unveiled at the Santiago Bernabeu.[1]

> *"I have nothing but praise for the boy. He is easily the best player in the world ... His stats are incredible. Strikes at goal, attempts on goal, raids into the penalty box, headers. It is all there. Absolutely astounding."*
>
> Sir Alex Ferguson, Manchester United manager[2]

While Ronaldo's seismic move to Spain hogged all the headlines in the close season, both in the UK and on the Continent, there was still plenty of activity elsewhere to fill the column inches, not least Ronaldo's teammate Carlos Tevez, who, controversially, chose to join rivals Manchester City for £25 million rather than extend his stay at Old Trafford.

"Welcome to Manchester"

A banner erected at the end of Deansgate in Manchester city centre – by Manchester City. It was a not-so-subtle dig at the fact that United's Old Trafford ground is actually outside the boundaries of Manchester.[3]

"Sometimes you have a noisy neighbour. They will always be noisy. You just have to get on with your life, put your television on and turn it up a bit louder."

Sir Alex Ferguson's pointed response.[4]

But the champions would finally have some competition in the shape of Chelsea. On 1 June 2009, the Blues appointed AC Milan manager Carlo Ancelotti as their fourth permanent manager in just 21 months. A double winner of the Champions League as a player and a coach, the 49-year-old Italian was precisely the kind of heavyweight manager Chelsea needed to drag them out of the torpor.

"I believe in teamwork. It is the most important thing to create a group that work together to build a dream. The players must have a strong organisation and strong discipline and strong motivation."

Carlo Ancelotti, new Chelsea manager[5]

One of his first signings is CSKA Moscow's Yuri Zhirkov, a player who fails to impress at the club's karaoke initiation ceremony.

"[He's] a Russian midfielder with a host of talents and just one shortcoming: he can't sing. He just makes a lot of noise … If you want to join the team, it's not enough just to sign a contract."

Carlo Ancelotti[6]

The season begins on 15 August and, under Ancelotti, Chelsea set the early pace, winning their first six matches on the spin. It's not such a great start for Manchester United, though. They lose to newly promoted Burnley in their second game as Robbie Blake's stunning volley steals the spoils.

"You just have to keep your eye on the ball until the last minute and release it. It either flies into Row Z or ends up in the back of the net. Luckily, it went in ... It was fantastic and something we will savour for a long time. But more than that, is nice to show people that we are willing to work and fight to stay in this division."

Robbie Blake, Burnley's hero of the hour.[7]

....

United would soon find their form. They win their next five games, including victories over Arsenal, Spurs and a dramatic 4-3 win over rivals Manchester City at Old Trafford in September, a match in which Michael Owen scored the winner deep into an inexplicable amount of stoppage time.

> "For sheer emotion and all the feelings that go with it after scoring a goal – that was right up there with the moments when you have the biggest surge of adrenaline."
>
> United's match-winner Michael Owen[8]

"You could say we feel frustrated, but robbed might be a better word. I'm not questioning the referee's integrity, I just don't know where he's got the seven minutes from."

City manager Mark Hughes. Another unwitting victim of 'Fergie Time'.[9]

....

There was controversy at the Stadium of Light when Sunderland hosted Liverpool on 17 October. With the game goalless, Sunderland striker Darren Bent struck a low shot towards the Liverpool goal, only to see it cannon off a rogue red beach ball, wrong-foot Liverpool goalkeeper Pepe Reina and find the back of the net.

> **"It was a strange goal. You don't get many deflections off beach balls."**
>
> Sunderland striker Darren Bent, a master of the understatement.[10]

"I'm the one who did it. I'm the one caught on camera. I'm so, so sorry. This is my worst, worst nightmare. When I got home I went into the garden and threw up. I was physically sick – and that's before the death threats started appearing on the internet the next day."

Callum Campbell, the 16-year-old Liverpool fan who threw the beach ball on the pitch.[11]

After their humiliation at Manchester City on Boxing Day 2008, Hull City returned to the City of Manchester Stadium in November. When midfielder Jimmy Bullard scores their equaliser in a 1-1 draw, he celebrates by sitting his teammates down in a circle and, like Phil Brown had done so publicly the previous season, wagging his finger at them all.

> **"It was a fantastic celebration. Great comedy is about timing. You could not have had a celebration like that, after a goal, unless it was at Eastlands and was in the goal in front of the Hull fans. The whole thing was timed to perfection."**
>
> Phil Brown, Hull City manager[12]

November also saw Spurs demolish Wigan Athletic 9-1 at White Hart Lane to become only the second team in Premier League history to score nine goals in one game. Man of the match was their striker Jermain Defoe, who netted five goals, all of which came in the second half. And to think it was only 1-0 to Tottenham at halftime.

> **"Adidas gave me a pair of green boots and I tried them on, but Clive Allen said I couldn't wear them, so I wore pinkish silver ones in the end and I go and score five."**
>
> Jermain Defoe on the secret of his successful haul.[13]

It's not all bad news for Wigan. At Stoke City soon after, their Honduran star Maynor Figueroa scoops the goal of the season award as he scores direct from a quickly taken free kick – from five yards inside his own half.

> **"Figueroa has got that quality and you see that he meant it – we will be seeing that goal for a long time."**
>
> Roberto Martinez, Wigan Athletic manager[14]

After a run of just one win in 10 games (a stretch that included seven consecutive draws), Manchester City manager Mark Hughes is a relieved man after his team hold on to beat Sunderland 4-3 at home. Two hours later, the club issues a statement announcing his departure. He is replaced by the Italian Roberto Mancini.

"I don't hold any resentment about that. The fact was I drew too many games and gave them the opportunity to go in a different direction. I think they would have done it sooner, but I didn't give them the opportunity because we won our first four games that season."

Mark Hughes reflects on his sacking at Manchester City.[15]

> **"This is our job. I am sorry for Mark. But when you start these jobs, this kind of situation is always possible. I was at Inter for four seasons and won seven trophies and then they sacked me. It's football."**
>
> Roberto Mancini, the new Manchester City manager[16]

Come the new year and Chelsea's title challenge was suddenly jeopardised by a scandal involving their skipper, John Terry. Newspapers reported how he had conducted an affair with Vanessa Perroncel, the girlfriend of his best friend and former Chelsea teammate Wayne Bridge.

"Chelsea, wherever you may be, don't leave your wife with John Terry."

Burnley fans have their say on the matter as Chelsea visit Turf Moor but John Terry has the last laugh, scoring a late winner in a 2-1 victory.[17]

On 31 January 2010, Sky Sports broadcast the first ever Premier League game to be shown live in 3D when they cover the match between Arsenal and Manchester United at the Emirates Stadium.

> *"You'll see every shot, every tackle and every save in a way you've never seen before. I'm sure it will revolutionise the way we watch live sports."*
>
> Sky Sports commentator Alan Parry. He was wrong.[18]

There's anger, controversy and recriminations at Stoke City in February as Potters' captain Ryan Shawcross shatters 19-year-old Arsenal midfielder Aaron Ramsey's leg in a reckless challenge. Shawcross is banned for three games while Ramsey is sidelined for nine months.

"I didn't see many bad tackles in the game but this one was horrendous. To lose a player of that quality at 19 years of age when he is just starting his career is just horrendous. It is difficult to accept."

Arsène Wenger, Arsenal manager[19]

Despite back-to-back defeats in the game against United and then away at Chelsea, Arsenal returned to form, winning six matches on the spin to top the table, albeit only for a day as United and Chelsea both overhauled them. But after a 1-1 draw with Birmingham City, the Gunners' title challenge faded badly and their return of just eight points from their final seven games saw them fall away, eventually finishing third.

But it was Chelsea, so long the season's front runners, that eased ahead as the campaign headed into April, reinforcing their superiority with a 2-1 win over their nearest challengers, Manchester United, at Old Trafford, thanks to a disputed goal by Didier Drogba.

"The linesman is right in front of Drogba and he gets it wrong. It was a poor, poor performance from the officials in a game of this magnitude."

Sir Alex Ferguson[20]

As the title race went to the final day, Chelsea held a one-point advantage over the reigning champions, Manchester United. Win against Wigan at Stamford Bridge and they would be champions, regardless of what United did at home to Stoke City.

As it transpired, United duly dispatched Stoke but their 4-0 win was in vain as Chelsea, inspired by a Didier Drogba hat trick, wrapped up the title in style, hammering Wigan 8-0 to take their third Premier League crown in true style.

"MORE THAN SPECIAL"

A banner in honour of Carlo Ancelotti, unfurled at the final whistle at Stamford Bridge.[21]

Drogba's hat trick gave him the season's Golden Boot with an impressive haul of 29 goals and took Chelsea's goal tally in their last 10 league games to an astonishing 39. Their season total of 103 goals, meanwhile, saw them become the first side since Tottenham in 1962/3 to reach a century of goals in the top division.

When they followed it by winning the FA Cup a week later, it was justification, in brilliant double-winning fashion, of the decision to change managers once more and appoint Carlo Ancelotti.

"I am lucky."

Carlo Ancelotti explains the secret of his success.[22]

Games Played: 38

Pos	Team	GD	Pts
1	Chelsea	+71	86
2	Manchester United	+58	85
3	Arsenal	+42	75
4	Tottenham Hotspur	+26	70
5	Manchester City	+28	67
6	Aston Villa	+13	64
7	Liverpool	+26	63
8	Everton	+11	61
9	Birmingham City	-9	50
10	Blackburn Rovers	-14	50
11	Stoke City	-14	47
12	Fulham	-7	46
13	Sunderland	-8	44
14	Bolton Wanderers	-25	39
15	Wolverhampton Wanderers	-24	38
16	Wigan Athletic	-42	36
17	West Ham United	-19	35
18	Burnley	-40	30
19	Hull City	-41	30
20	Portsmouth	-32	19

CHAMPIONS: Chelsea

RUNNERS-UP: Manchester United

RELEGATED: Burnley, Hull City, Portsmouth

PROMOTED: West Bromwich Albion, Newcastle United, Blackpool

TOP GOALSCORER: Didier Drogba, Chelsea – 29

PLAYER OF THE SEASON: Wayne Rooney, Manchester United

MANAGER OF THE SEASON: Harry Redknapp, Tottenham Hotspur

DID YOU KNOW? *Wigan Athletic became the first team in Premier League history to lose two games by eight goals in a season when they lost 8–0 to Chelsea and 9–1 to Spurs.*

Top of the League

As the top flight hosted all four major West Midlands clubs – Aston Villa, Birmingham City, West Bromwich Albion and Wolverhampton Wanderers – for the first time in its history, the league's big clubs began to exert their superior spending power in a bid to keep pace with pre-championship favourites Chelsea and Manchester United.

With Rafa Benitez relieved of his duties at Anfield and a new manager, Roy Hodgson, at the helm, Liverpool take Raul Meireles from Porto and Christian Poulsen from Juventus, while Spurs sign the Dutchman Rafael van der Vaart from Real Madrid.

But it's Manchester City that seem intent on launching their most serious Premier League title challenge to date, adding the Spanish international David Silva, Barcelona's Ivorian star Yaya Toure and Lazio's Aleksandar Kolarov to their squad, for a combined total of almost £60 million.

When the season begins, the champions, Chelsea, complete with their new Brazilian midfielder Ramires in their ranks, pick up where they left off in 2009/10. They win their opening five games and rack up the goals with back-to-back 6-0 victories over West Bromwich Albion and Wigan Athletic.

"It is difficult to know why people think that Arsenal play the better football. Even when we finished top, people still said Arsenal played better than us."

Chelsea's Florent Malouda on changing people's perception of his team.[1]

There's a breath of fresh air in the Premier League as Blackpool make their debut in the division. Led by their charismatic, straight-talking manager, Ian Holloway, they win their first game against Wigan 4-0 to top the table, albeit briefly. The following week, they are hammered 6-0 at Arsenal.

> **"I may be in a bit of a Skoda garage rather than a Mercedes garage, but I am telling you some old bangers don't half polish up great."**
>
> Blackpool manager Ian Holloway, defiant in defeat.[2]

Manchester United, seeking a record 19th title, also make an impressive start to their campaign. Indeed, the Red Devils would remain unbeaten until a shock 2-1 defeat at Wolves in early February. At times they are untouchable, a 3-2 triumph over rivals Liverpool, a 7-1 win over Blackburn and a 5-0 victory over Birmingham proving to be the high points.

Key to their success is their Bulgarian striker Dimitar Berbatov, who scores hat tricks against Birmingham and Liverpool and five against Blackburn.

> *"He [Berbatov] gets criticised unfairly because he looks laid back and looks as though he doesn't care. But that's not necessarily the case. I had a player at Bolton called Nicolas Anelka who everyone thought was sulky. But when I worked with him I realised that was wrong. He wasn't like that at all."*
>
> Sam Allardyce, Blackburn Rovers manager[3]

As Manchester United's progress continues unabated, speculation is rife that manager Sir Alex Ferguson is considering stepping down at the end of the season. It's a rumour he's keen to quash.

> **"Retirement is for young people; they can do something else. I'm a phenomenon."**
>
> Sir Alex Ferguson, Manchester United manager[4]

United also have to deal with a bolt from the blue in the shape of a transfer request from unsettled star striker Wayne Rooney, with reports even linking him to a move to neighbours Manchester City.

"Join City and you're dead."

Graffiti in Manchester city centre[5]

"Sometimes you look in a field and see a cow and you think it's a better cow than the one you you've got in your own field ... It never really works out that way."

Manchester United manager Sir Alex Ferguson on why Wayne Rooney should stay at Old Trafford.[6]

Two days later, Rooney signs a new five-year contract at Old Trafford that doubles his wages and makes him the highest-paid player in the club's history.

"I'm sure the fans over the last week have felt let down by what they've read and seen. The fans have been upset but my message to them is that I care for the club. I just want it to continue to be successful."

Wayne Rooney on his speedy u-turn.[7]

After a dire first half to the season that saw them lose nine times, Liverpool sack manager Roy Hodgson, his last game being a 3-1 defeat away at Blackburn. Out of the FA Cup, out of the League Cup and sitting 12th in the table, the club turn to former player and manager Kenny Dalglish to steady the ship.

"We had a lovely dinner with Kenny [Dalglish], his wife Marina and son Paul. I understood half of what he said and just nodded when I couldn't understand."

Tom Werner, Liverpool chairman. Werner's Fenway Sports Group had taken over at Anfield on 15 October 2010.[8]

After 18 years and 602 games for Manchester United, 35-year-old defender Gary Neville retires. He plays his final game in a 2-1 victory over West Bromwich Albion.

"I have been a Manchester United fan all my life and fulfilled every dream I've ever had. I have played in the most incredible football teams, playing with some of the best players in the world as well as against them, and I have been lucky to be a part of the team's achievements and the club's great success ... There have also been so many great players that I have had the privilege to train and play alongside. The experiences we've shared will be with me for the rest of my life."

Gary Neville[9]

An otherwise quiet winter transfer window is enlivened by a flurry of activity on the deadline day, 31 January. As Liverpool sell their Spanish striker Fernando Torres to Chelsea for a British record £50 million, they replace him with not one but two new strikers, Newcastle's Andy Carroll (£35 million) and Ajax's Luis Suarez (£22.7 million). Chelsea, meanwhile, also secure the services of highly rated Benfica defender David Luiz (£21 million).

> *"I'm staggered just like the rest of Newcastle fans. It's an incredible amount of money, you have to say that, for a guy who's scored – what is it? – 14 goals and had half a season in the Premier League."*
>
> Newcastle fan and BBC football pundit Alan Shearer on the Andy Carroll deal.[10]

The game of the season takes place at St James' Park on 5 February when Newcastle United host title challengers Arsenal. It's the classic game of two halves as Arsenal race into a 4-0 lead within half an hour of the kick-off but are forced to share the spoils as the Magpies storm back, scoring four times in the final 22 minutes to take a point.

"Our fans will remember this for a long time. When we went four goals down I thought the house might come down, but in the end we sent 51,000 Geordies home relatively happy."

Alan Pardew, Newcastle manager[11]

> **"We panicked a little bit in the second half, we have dropped two points, but psychologically the damage is bigger. We have a very disappointed dressing room."**
>
> Arsène Wenger, Arsenal manager[12]

A week later, the two Manchester clubs faced each other at Old Trafford, with United top of the table and City in third place. It would be a game settled by what would go on to be voted the best Premier League goal in the competition's 20-year history. With 12 minutes to play, the game was poised at 1-1 when United attacked down the right, their Portuguese winger Nani swinging a cross in from the flank.

In a flash, Wayne Rooney arches his back and launches himself acrobatically into an overhead kick that catches everyone by surprise and thumps into the top corner of Joe Hart's net.

It was a goal worthy of winning any game, yet alone a Manchester derby.

"We were beaten by a moment of pure genius."

Roberto Mancini, Manchester City boss[13]

> "I can't ever remember a better goal at Old Trafford. In terms of the execution of it, you will never see a better goal than that. It reminded me of Denis Law, although whether Denis ever put them in with such ferocity, I'm not so sure."
>
> Sir Alex Ferguson, Manchester United manager[14]

While Roberto Mancini conceded that City's title challenge was all but over – they were now eight points behind their neighbours – United's march to another title hit a bump in the road in early March, losing first to Chelsea and then, five days later, to Liverpool where the Dutchman Dirk Kuyt stole the show with a hat trick in a 3-1 win at Anfield.

"Can we play you every week?"

Never ones to miss a chance to taunt United, the Kop launch into full voice in the win over their rivals at Anfield.[15]

Meanwhile, in west London there's uproar at Fulham where the club's owner, Mohamed Al-Fayed, unveils a 2.3-metre-high statue of the late Michael Jackson outside Craven Cottage. In 1999, Jackson had been a guest of Al-Fayed at the club and had watched Fulham play Wigan. Now, two years after the performer's death, Al-Fayed had decided to commemorate his friendship with the so-called 'King of Pop'.

"If some stupid fans don't understand and appreciate such a gift this guy gave to the world they can go to hell. I don't want them to be fans. If they don't understand and don't believe in things I believe in they can go to Chelsea, they can go to anywhere else."

Mohamed Al-Fayed, Fulham owner[16]

Manchester United's defeat to Liverpool and, later, a 1-0 reverse at Arsenal did little to dent their title charge. They had occupied the top slot in the table since late November and, as they had on many occasions before, repelled all pretenders to their throne with ruthless efficiency.

With three games to play, the championship effectively comes down to United's home game with closest challengers Chelsea. They don't let it slip. One goal to the good after just 37 seconds through Javier Hernandez, they add another through their Player of the Season Nemanja Vidic before halftime, and though Frank Lampard pulls one back for the reigning champions it's now all but over.

A week later, Manchester United duly wrap up the title with a 1-1 draw at Blackburn Rovers. Another season, another Premier League triumph. They finish the season in style, beating Blackpool 4-2 at a jubilant Old Trafford, consigning the Seasiders to relegation after just one season in the Premier League. They also go on to reach the final of the Champions League but, once again, are beaten by Barcelona.

> "What a season ... All these last-minute goals! I don't know how you survive. I'll be stretchered out of here at the end of the day!"
>
> Sir Alex Ferguson addresses the Old Trafford crowd after the game.[17]

When Alex Ferguson took over at Manchester United in 1986 he knew what he had to do to make Manchester United the greatest club in the world.

"My greatest challenge was knocking Liverpool right off their f**** perch."**

Sir Alex Ferguson[18]

And with a record 19th top-flight title, eclipsing Liverpool's record, to celebrate at Old Trafford, it's safe to say that Fergie had done precisely that.

Games Played: 38

Pos	Team	GD	Pts
1	Manchester United	+41	80
2	Chelsea	+36	71
3	Manchester City	+27	71
4	Arsenal	+29	68
5	Tottenham Hotspur	+9	62
6	Liverpool	+15	58
7	Everton	+6	54
8	Fulham	+6	49
9	Aston Villa	-11	48
10	Sunderland	-11	47
11	West Bromwich Albion	-15	47
12	Newcastle United	-1	46
13	Stoke City	-2	46
14	Bolton Wanderers	-4	46
15	Blackburn Rovers	-13	43
16	Wigan Athletic	-21	42
17	Wolverhampton Wanderers	-20	40
18	Birmingham City	-21	39
19	Blackpool	-23	39
20	West Ham United	-27	33

CHAMPIONS: Manchester United

RUNNERS-UP: Chelsea

RELEGATED: Birmingham City, Blackpool, West Ham United

PROMOTED: Swansea City, Norwich City, Queens Park Rangers

TOP GOALSCORERS: Dimitar Berbatov (Manchester United), Carlos Tevez (Manchester City) – 20

PLAYER OF THE SEASON: Gareth Bale, Tottenham Hotspur

MANAGER OF THE SEASON: Sir Alex Ferguson, Manchester United

DID YOU KNOW? *There was an average of 2.80 goals per game in the 2010/11 season, the highest ratio in Premier League history to date.*

The Noisy Neighbours Leave It Late

The 20th season of the Premier League began in bright sunshine on Saturday 13 August – and ended in the most astonishing manner imaginable.

It was a season of rare vintage. A record 1066 goals would be scored over the course of the campaign, with Aston Villa's Marc Albrighton also bagging the 20,000th goal in the competition's history in a 2-1 defeat at Arsenal.

As Manchester City seek to improve on their third-place finish in 2010/11, they sign Atletico Madrid's striker Sergio Aguero for £38 million and the Argentinian makes an immediate impact, coming on as a substitute and scoring twice on his Premier League debut in a 4-0 win over Swansea.

"They brought [Sergio] Aguero on, and he cost more than our stadium."

Brendan Rodgers, Swansea manager[1]

Newcastle United would also start well with a new signing, the stylish French star Yohan Cabaye, impressing in midfield. In his first full season at the club, manager Alan Pardew guides the Magpies to an unbeaten 11-match streak.

> **"I hope the Toon enjoy it tonight. We are a new team, we didn't expect to be on this run but we are enjoying it."**
>
> Alan Pardew, Newcastle manager[2]

Having won their first two games, Manchester United welcomed their old enemy, Arsenal, to Old Trafford at the end of August. But as soon as United's first goal went in from Danny Welbeck, it opened the floodgates for a result nobody could have predicted. Ashley Young weighed in with two goals while a hat trick from Wayne Rooney took him over 150 goals for the club and United emerge as scarcely credible 8-2 winners.

"It was painful for us."

Arsenal's manager Arsène Wenger, a man whose position was under pressure before the result against United.[3]

"The last rites were read. Hold the obituary page."

Henry Winter with *The Daily Telegraph*'s match report.[4]

When they follow up with convincing wins over Bolton (5-0) and Chelsea (3-1), United head into October unbeaten and top of the table, their title defence well and truly on track. Their main challengers, however, are near neighbours Manchester City, who are also unbeaten as the two sides square up at Old Trafford on 23 October.

But just as United's crushing win over Arsenal had come from nowhere, so too was City's breathtaking 6-1 victory, a result that's United's worst home defeat since February 1955.

"United had dominated for decades in Manchester and we changed history. The 6-1 at Old Trafford remains an indelible memory. Alex Ferguson was a bit angry that day."

Roberto Mancini, Manchester City manager[5]

"WHY ALWAYS ME?"

City's Mario Balotelli reveals his t-shirt after scoring, a reference to the endless media reports on his private life. The unpredictable Italian had arrived at Manchester City in the summer from Inter Milan to reunite with his former manager Roberto Mancini.[6]

"I think the fact that Alex Ferguson rested [referee] Howard Webb had a lot to do with the result."

Noel Gallagher, Manchester City fan and Oasis founder[7]

If United's form prior to the game was typically consistent, then City's before and after was simply sensational. They remained unbeaten until a 2-1 reverse at Chelsea on 12 December. In that period they won 12 of their 14 games, scoring a scarcely believable 49 goals in the process.

But there's another story hogging the headlines. On 12 October, during an ill-tempered game between Liverpool and Manchester United, Reds' striker Luis Suarez is accused by the United defender Patrice Evra of racially abusing him repeatedly. Though Liverpool back their striker in the following weeks – the players even wear t-shirts supporting him before their match against Wigan – he is eventually found guilty by the Football Association, banned for eight matches and fined £40,000.

"These things happen in football, in the heat of the moment. They leave someone looking bad. Now we have to see how the matter is decided and then, for him as much as me, we will have things clear. And wherever the fault lies, we are going to have to say sorry."

Luis Suarez[8]

In the same game, United forward Wayne Rooney is taunted mercilessly by Liverpool fans as they get their first view of his recent hair transplant.

"Who's the Scouser in the wig?"

The Kop, in fine form.[9]

Despite a difficult start to their campaign, where they lost 3-0 to Manchester United and then 5-1 to Manchester City, Tottenham also stake their claim to the title. Harry Redknapp's attacking side thrash Liverpool 4-0 (with Emmanuel Adebayor scoring twice on his home debut) and beat Arsenal 2-1 on their way to an 11-game unbeaten run. Even a narrow defeat at Stoke in December fails to halt their progress. Indeed, it's the only match they lose until they go down 3-2 at Manchester City on 22 January.

The win means City have taken 58 points from a possible 60 in their last 20 home league games and won the last 15 in a row.

It's not long before the Suarez and Evra affair raises its head again. As Manchester United and Liverpool line up before their game at Old Trafford, United skipper Patrice Evra holds out his hand in an act of reconciliation but is ignored by the Uruguayan striker, prompting another angry exchange.

"Suarez is a disgrace to Liverpool Football Club. He should not be allowed to play for Liverpool again. He could have caused a riot."

Manchester United manager Alex Ferguson, whose side went on to win 2-1 and top the table.[10]

> "I think you're bang out of order to blame Luis Suarez for anything that happened here today."
>
> Kenny Dalglish continues to back his striker.[11]

Chelsea's failure to mount a sustained title challenge sees their manager Andrew Villas-Boas removed from his office in February. Assistant manager Roberto Di Matteo is appointed as caretaker manager until the end of the season, and while the club fail to make the top four, they do qualify for the Champions League by winning a remarkable final against Bayern Munich in the Germans' own stadium. The Italian also guides Chelsea to an FA Cup win. Not bad for a caretaker coach.

Football pales into insignificance on 17 March when, 43 minutes into Spurs' FA Cup tie against Bolton Wanderers, the visitors' midfielder Fabrice Muamba collapses on the pitch, the result of sudden cardiac arrest. The England Under-21 player is given CPR on the pitch and a defibrillator is also used. It later transpires that Muamba's heart stops for 78 minutes before he is revived in hospital and though he recovers, he is unable to play again. The match, meanwhile, is abandoned.

"PRAY 4 MUAMBA"

Chelsea's Gary Cahill reveals a supportive t-shirt, having scored for Chelsea. The defender played with Muamba at Bolton for two and a half years.[12]

"I just felt myself falling through the air then felt two big thumps as my head hit the ground in front of me then that was it. Blackness, nothing. I was dead."

Bolton midfielder Fabrice Muamba, who retired from playing in August 2012.[13]

With a couple of months left of the season, it was clear that there were only two teams vying for the title, with Arsenal, Spurs and Newcastle too far behind to mount a challenge. Ominously, Manchester United move into pole position, a run of eight wins on the spin putting them in touching distance of retaining their title.

Manchester City, meanwhile, hit the ropes, winning just one of five and losing to Swansea and Arsenal, a game that sees Mario Balotelli, a player once described as 'unmanageable' by his former boss José Mourinho, sent off for a series of mad (and maddening) tackles.

"I don't have any words about his behaviour ... but he needs to change."

City boss Roberto Mancini lays it on the line for Mario Balotelli.[14]

Somehow, Manchester City contrive to turn a five-point lead into an eight-point deficit in little more than a month.

"In football it's never finished."

City boss Roberto Mancini[15]

But there's a glimmer of hope for the Citizens. As City win five consecutive games, it's United that falter, losing to Wigan, drawing 4-4 with Everton and losing to City themselves at the end of April. Though United recover to beat Swansea in their penultimate game, it leaves both sides locked on 86 points going into the final match of the season. Crucially, though, it's City that have the superior goal difference. If they can match United's result at Sunderland in their home game against QPR, they'll be champions.

But it doesn't quite go to plan. After 66 minutes they are losing 2-1, despite QPR having Joey Barton sent off, while at Sunderland's Stadium of Light United are in control and, it seems, heading for the championship.

Desperate for something to change, City boss Roberto Mancini throws on Mario Balotelli and Edin Dzeko, but City are still trailing as the game enters five minutes of injury time. In the 93rd minute, City have hope as Dzeko heads home a David Silva corner. With nerves shredded and United fans already celebrating another title triumph after a 1-0 win, City mount one last assault on the QPR goal.

As the ball reaches Balotelli in the box, he squeezes it wide to Sergio Aguero, who takes a touch and, improbably, lashes a fierce drive past Paddy Kenny and inside the near post.

Cue bedlam.

"Aguerooooooooo … I swear you'll never see anything like this ever again. So watch it, drink it in … two goals in added time from Manchester City to snatch the title away from Manchester United."

Martin Tyler and his now legendary commentary on Sky Sports.[16]

"I wish I could tell you how I did it, but I can't."

Sergio Aguero, City's match, and title, winner.[17]

"After this I feel 90 years old. I think we have changed the history of this club, and for this we should be proud. I think it was a crazy finish for a crazy season. I have never seen a final day like this. The best team won the title."

Roberto Mancini, Manchester City manager[18]

> *"Everyone expected City to win. They had to do it against 10 men for half an hour and they had five minutes of injury time to help them, but at the end of the day, on behalf of everyone at Manchester United, I congratulate Manchester City on winning the league."*

Shell-shocked praise from Sir Alex Ferguson, the man who invented 'Fergie time'.[19]

It is the first time in the Premier League's history that goal difference has determined the Premier League winners and ends Manchester City's 44-year wait to win the top-flight title, an era in which they had been forced to sit by and watch as rivals United won almost everything in sight. United, meanwhile, had won the highest number of points (89) in Premier League history without winning the title.

"Miracles do happen in Manchester – on this side of the road this time."

Vincent Kompany, Manchester City's captain and the PFA Player of the Year.[20]

Games Played: 38

Pos	Team	GD	Pts
1	Manchester City	+64	89
2	Manchester United	+56	89
3	Arsenal	+25	70
4	Tottenham Hotspur	+25	69
5	Newcastle United	+5	65
6	Chelsea	+19	64
7	Everton	+10	56
8	Liverpool	+7	52
9	Fulham	-3	52
10	West Bromwich Albion	-7	47
11	Swansea	-7	47
12	Norwich	-14	47
13	Sunderland	-1	45
14	Stoke City	-17	45
15	Wigan Athletic	-20	43
16	Aston Villa	-16	38
17	Queens Park Rangers	-23	37
18	Bolton Wanderers	-31	36
19	Blackburn Rovers	-30	31
20	Wolverhampton Wanderers	-42	25

CHAMPIONS: Manchester City

RUNNERS-UP: Manchester United

RELEGATED: Bolton Wanderers, Blackburn Rovers, Wolverhampton Wanderers

PROMOTED: West Ham United, Southampton, Reading

TOP GOALSCORER: Robin Van Persie, Manchester United – 30

PLAYER OF THE SEASON: Robin Van Persie, Manchester United

MANAGER OF THE SEASON: Alan Pardew, Newcastle United

DID YOU KNOW? *When Joey Barton was sent off against Manchester City on the final day of the season, it was QPR's ninth red card of the season, equalling the Premier League record set by Sunderland in 2009/10.*

PREMIER LEAGUE 2012/13

End of an Era

After the electrifying climax to the 2011/12 season, the new Premier League campaign saw Manchester United eager to regain the title they lost to rivals City just three months earlier, not least because this, finally, would be manager Sir Alex Ferguson's last season in charge at Old Trafford.

While United aimed to give Ferguson the send-off he clearly deserved, there were managerial changes galore before the season got underway. At Anfield, Liverpool hire Brendan Rodgers as their new manager, with the Dane Michael Laudrup replacing him at Swansea.

"It really doesn't matter if we finish 10th or 14th. Who will remember if we have 43 or 48 points? It's overall – how did they play? If you asked the people on the street in Swansea, 'What do you prefer, 10th and changing style of play or 14th and remain the same style?' The answer is obvious."

Michael Laudrup, new Swansea coach[1]

Spurs, meanwhile, appoint Andre Villas-Boas, the Portuguese coach who had endured a brief and unsuccessful stint at Chelsea, while Aston Villa recruit Paul Lambert and Norwich City name Chris Hughton as their new coach.

West Bromwich Albion, meanwhile, are forced into a managerial change as Roy Hodgson takes up an offer to become manager of England, giving Steve Clarke the opportunity to test himself in his first permanent job as a manager.

There's a clutch of stellar names that arrive in the Premier League, too, with Chelsea's Eden Hazard, Arsenal's Santi Cazorla and Olivier Giroud and Manchester United's Shinji Kagawa all landing in the Premier League. It's not United's only key signing, however, as they lure Robin Van Persie away from Arsenal for £24 million.

The season begins on 18 August, with newly promoted teams Reading, Southampton (after a seven-year absence from the top flight) and West Ham (via the play-offs) all joining the Premier League party. It's Chelsea that make the early running, winning seven of their first eight games and remaining unbeaten – until they come up against Manchester United on 28 October.

In a pulsating game at Stamford Bridge, Chelsea rallied from two goals down to pull level but then lost Branislav Ivanovic and Fernando Torres to red cards, the latter receiving a second yellow card for diving even though he had been fouled by Jonny Evans. The Blues' misery was compounded by a controversial stoppage-time winner from United substitute Javier Hernandez, who appeared to be offside as he scored.

> *"It is a shame a game like this had to be decided in that manner by officials ... It is a shame because it was a good game of football with two good teams and the officials ruined it."*
>
> Chelsea boss Roberto Di Matteo is none too impressed with referee Mark Clattenburg and his assistants.[2]

"We've never got breaks down here and had some terrible decisions against us in the last few years. But today we have got a little break for the goal."

United manager Sir Alex Ferguson, ever gracious.[3]

In the last week of October there's a new Premier League record set as the game between Manchester City and Swansea lasts 103 minutes, as two serious injuries to Micah Richards and Michel Vorm require lengthy treatment.

It's a solid start to the season for West Ham United, who find themselves within touching distance of the top four. It's a run of form that both delights and irks their manager, Sam Allardyce, who feels he doesn't get the credit he deserves.

> **"I won't ever be going to a top-four club because I'm not called Allardici, just Allardyce."**
>
> Sam Allardyce on his chances of getting a job at one of the Premier League's so-called bigger clubs.[4]

As the season progresses, it's Manchester United that set the pace, winning 14 of their first 16 games to take a commanding lead in the Premier League. It's the kind of form that the other teams simply can't live with and the likes of Chelsea, Manchester City and Arsenal struggle to keep pace with Alex Ferguson's side.

Seemingly determined to make amends for the near-miss of the 2011/12 season, Manchester United show real resolve in their bid to wrest the title from neighbours City. Three times they are behind to Newcastle and each time they come back before scoring an injury-time winner through Javier Hernandez. It's classic 'Fergie Time' stuff from the Red Devils.

In late November, the morning after a 3-0 defeat at Juventus in the Champions League, Chelsea sack their manager, Roberto Di Matteo, despite winning the Champions League and the FA Cup in his 262-day reign and topping the table in the early weeks of the season. He is replaced, on an interim basis, by former Liverpool manager Rafa Benitez.

"The team's recent performances and results have not been good enough and the owner and the board felt that a change was necessary now to keep the club moving in the right direction as we head into a vitally important part of the season."

Chelsea FC statement[5]

"THE INTERIM ONE – NOT WANTED, NEVER WANTED, RAFA OUT!"

"RAFA BENITEZ – WE'RE JUST NOT THAT IN TER IM"

A selection of Chelsea fans' banners[6]

Spurs, meanwhile, welcome Liverpool to White Hart Lane and history is made as Gareth Bale scores, assists, scores an own goal and is booked in a 2-1 win to become the only player in Premier League history to do so.

"At the moment he's doing extremely well for Spurs and we are absolutely amazed with what he can do for us ... But Tottenham as a club want to keep him here as long as we can but we understand players like this have propositions, have a market which is the nature of the game."

Tottenham manager Andre Villas-Boas sings Gareth Bale's praises.[7]

By December, Rafa Benitez was starting to get real results with his Chelsea team. First, he had shored up the defence, finally keeping clean sheets for the first time last September and scoring freely at the other end. They beat Nordsjaelland 6-1 in the Champions League, won 3-1 at Sunderland and took out Leeds 5-1 in the League Cup. Then, on 23 December, they destroyed Aston Villa, scoring eight unanswered goals from eight different goalscorers.

"We got beaten up pretty badly, from start to finish."

Paul Lambert, Aston Villa manager[8]

Villa aren't the only side on the wrong end of a festive thumping. At the Emirates Stadium, Arsenal put seven past Newcastle, running out 7-3 winners with Theo Walcott scoring three and setting up two others.

"I've been consistent in patches this season."

Arsenal's Theo Walcott[9]

As Martin O'Neill's Sunderland struggle near the foot of the Premier League table, the Black Cats' manager is relieved of his duties at the Stadium of Light, an eight-game winless run proving to be the final straw. The next day, Sunderland announce his replacement, the controversial Italian Paolo Di Canio.

"I know other Romans came 2000 years ago. They conquered the North East and were here for 100 years. Maybe after two months it will be 'Di Canio f*** off, bye bye Paolo.' It can happen but I'm sure it won't."

Paolo Di Canio in typically bullish mood upon arrival at Sunderland in 2013.[10]

"Often I refer to it as management by hand grenade. Paolo would chuck a hand grenade and I would do the repair work at the end, like the Red Cross."

Nick Watkins, who worked as Di Canio's chief executive when he was manager at Swindon Town.[11]

As the season drew to its inevitable end – the title was all but over – it was clear that only one player would win the Player of the Year award, Tottenham's Gareth Bale. The Welshman had scored 21 goals in the Premier League, many of which were outstanding long-range efforts. A case in point was the away game at West Ham, where Bale hammered an injury-time winner home to give Spurs a thrilling 3-2 victory.

> "Gaz is up there with Ronaldo and Messi in terms of ability ... Some of the things he does would make Ronaldo blush."
>
> Bale's Tottenham teammate Michael Dawson[12]

In mid-April, Liverpool play out an entertaining 2-2 draw with Chelsea at Anfield but the game is remembered for something other than the quality of the match as the Uruguayan striker Luis Suarez bites Chelsea defender Branislav Ivanovic. It's the second time in his career that Suarez has bitten an opponent – and, remarkably, it won't be the last.

> **"There is no precedent for what Suarez did – other than he's done it before."**
>
> Danny Mills, Radio 5 Live analyst[13]

> **"I made my own views clear just as a dad watching the game. I've got a seven-year-old son who just loves watching football and when players behave like this it just sets the most appalling example to young people in our country."**
>
> Prime Minister David Cameron, after Suarez received a 10-game ban for his bite on Branislav Ivanovic.[14]

They may have had their best player and highest scorer sidelined but Liverpool showed no signs of suffering. In the next game, they pummelled Newcastle United at St James' Park 6-0. It was the first time that the Magpies had lost a match in the highest division by six or more goals since they were beaten 7-1 by Blackburn back in September 1925. It's also the first time that a Premier League side has fielded seven foreign players all from the same nation which, in Newcastle's case, is France.

> *"To come to St James' Park and win six-nil is very impressive. It's been a traumatic week for the football club. We accepted that. Luis did wrong, he takes his punishment and we move on. We had to move on with a performance."*
>
> Brendan Rodgers, Liverpool manager[15]

> "We haven't become a bad staff or a bad set of players overnight. We need to roll our sleeves up ... but it was an awful performance."
>
> Newcastle boss Alan Pardew[16]

While Liverpool finished the season strongly, Manchester United's cakewalk to yet another Premier League crown is finally confirmed with a convincing 3-0 victory over Aston Villa on 22 April, a game in which striker Robin Van Persie scores a phenomenal hat trick, including a spectacular volley that's named Goal of the Season.

> "Van Persie making a trademark run again and what a ball to pick him out ... and what a finish! A magnificent goal by Robin Van Persie!"
>
> Peter Drury's TV commentary[17]

Having watched neighbours Manchester City take the title with virtually the last kick of the season the year before, United prove, yet again, that they are the best side of their generation. They win the title – their 20th –with four games to spare and with 89 points, 11 clear of Manchester City.

> *"I had to wait so long for my first title. It is a great feeling. It is a fantastic team and fantastic players. It is a championship for every single one of them. The staff, the managers, the physios. This is our 20th title, it is deserved."*
>
> Robin Van Persie, United's Golden Boot winner.[18]

There are mixed emotions at Wigan Athletic where, just three days after they upset the odds by beating overwhelming favourites Manchester City in the FA Cup final at Wembley, they lose 4-1 at Arsenal and are relegated from the Premier League, joining QPR and Reading in the drop.

"I can't quite believe it. I know from the outside relegation was a possibility, but I never thought it would happen ... It is difficult to describe my feelings because even now it is a shock. We are not a team that deserves to be in the bottom three."

Wigan manager Roberto Martinez, who lost his job soon after.[19]

In his last game in charge of Manchester United, 21 years, 13 titles, 38 trophies and 1500 games after he started at the club, Sir Alex Ferguson takes his all-conquering side to West Bromwich Albion where, despite going 3-0 up, the champions are pegged back by a Romelu Lukaku hat trick, eventually drawing the game 5-5. It's the highest-scoring draw in Premier League history.

"It was a great finale. Sir Alex told me it's the first time one of his teams has surrendered a three-goal lead, so credit has to go to my players for that. I think he will enjoy his retirement. People will remember that game for years to come. It's a great tribute to him."

Steve Clarke, West Brom manager[20]

"Sir Alex is going to be such a big, big, big hole to replace."

And a less eloquent tribute from his former captain, Steve Bruce.[21]

Ferguson isn't the only boss to bid farewell to his club. Despite the uproar that greeted his appointment at Stamford Bridge, Rafa Benitez ends his short stay in charge of Chelsea by leading them to victory in the Europa League final as the Blues beat Benfica in Amsterdam. Respect, albeit grudging, is due.

"I think it's sad to think we are now 'a success' when we have been doing our jobs for six or seven months. It would have changed nothing if we'd won or lost this final in terms of what we have been trying to do ... But we did win, so hopefully people will say: 'Yes, it's not bad.'"

Rafa Benitez, departing Chelsea manager[22]

Games Played: 38

Pos	Team	GD	Pts
1	Manchester United	+43	89
2	Manchester City	+32	78
3	Chelsea	+36	75
4	Arsenal	+35	73
5	Tottenham Hotspur	+20	72
6	Everton	+15	63
7	Liverpool	+28	61
8	West Bromwich Albion	-4	49
9	Swansea City	-4	46
10	West Ham United	-8	46
11	Norwich City	-17	44
12	Fulham	-10	43
13	Stoke City	-11	42
14	Southampton	-11	41
15	Aston Villa	-22	41
16	Newcastle United	-23	41
17	Sunderland	-13	39
18	Wigan Athletic	-26	36
19	Reading	-30	28
20	Queens Park Rangers	-30	25

CHAMPIONS: Manchester United

RUNNERS-UP: Manchester City

RELEGATED: Wigan Athletic, Reading, Queens Park Rangers

PROMOTED: Crystal Palace, Hull City, Cardiff City

TOP GOALSCORER: Robin Van Persie, Manchester United – 26

PLAYER OF THE SEASON: Gareth Bale, Tottenham Hotspur

MANAGER OF THE SEASON: Sir Alex Ferguson, Manchester United

DID YOU KNOW? *Manchester United became only the fourth side in Premier League history to not concede a single penalty kick in a season. The others were Newcastle United in 1995/6, Bolton Wanderers in 1997/8 and Arsenal in 1999/2000.*

Liverpool Fall Short

It's 1 July, and it's a momentous day at Old Trafford as David Moyes officially takes over as manager of Manchester United. The former Everton boss is given a six-year contract and comes personally recommended by his predecessor, Sir Alex Ferguson.

"All I can do is what David Moyes has done before."

So says David Moyes, which, at Everton, was no trophies in 11 years in charge.[1]

"THE CHOSEN ONE"

A new banner emerges in Old Trafford's Stretford End.[2]

....

It's not the only high-profile hot seat that's filled during the close season. Having won the Europa League in his temporary stay in charge at Chelsea, Rafa Benitez steps aside to allow José Mourinho's return to Stamford Bridge, six years after he was sacked.

> "We are getting together at a great moment for us both, so I think we are ready to marry again and be happy and successful."
>
> José Mourinho, new Chelsea manager[3]

"José Mourinho is living, swaggering proof that when you fall in love with yourself there is every chance it will prove a lifelong romance."

James Lawton, *The Independent*[4]

On the playing front, Spurs allow Gareth Bale to leave for Real Madrid for a world record transfer fee of £86 million, and then promptly spend the money on a clutch of players including Christian Eriksen, Erik Lamela, Roberto Soldado, Paulinho and Nacer Chadli, some of whom perform better than others.

Manchester City splash out £90 million on five new players including the Brazilian Fernandinho, Fiorentina's Stevan Jovetic and Sevilla duo Jesus Navas and Alvaro Negredo, while Chelsea add Brazil's Willian, German international Andre Schurrle and former Barcelona star Samuel Eto'o to their already impressive roster.

West Ham, meanwhile, end Andy Carroll's Liverpool nightmare, picking him up for less than half what the Reds paid for him. The 24-year-old had been on loan at the Hammers but put pen to paper on a permanent six-year deal.

> *"The fans, the lads and the club itself have been great to me, and what I wanted to do was come back here and play football. Since the end of the season I've had a lot of time to think, I've missed it and that's why I'm back."*
>
> West Ham's Andy Carroll[5]

The season begins on Saturday 17 August, and although they lose their opener at home to Aston Villa, Arsenal's early form sees them seize the initiative in the title race. They win 11 of their following 13 games, suffering just one defeat, a narrow 1-0 reverse at Manchester United in which their former striker Robin Van Persie scores – and then celebrates with the kind of gusto to suggest he used to play for Spurs.

> **"Of course it's strange because for me he's an Arsenal man."**
>
> Arsène Wenger, Arsenal boss[6]

Just 13 games after his appointment and amid reports of a huge training ground bust-up with his players, Sunderland decide that Paolo Di Canio isn't the man for them after all. The team, yet again, are bottom of the table with just one point from five games.

"Me walk away? What? Never. I always believe that I am the best manager in the world. Why should I have to walk out? I have been working 24 hours a day. The players have to adapt to me, to one person. I cannot be a fake Di Canio."

Paolo Di Canio, before his last game in charge, a 3-0 defeat against West Bromwich Albion.[7]

"The players think they know everything, diet, how long they train, they are never happy."

And Di Canio, a year after being sacked at Sunderland.[8]

On 2 November, just 13 seconds into the game, Stoke goalkeeper Asmir Begovic punts a clearance 91.9 metres down the field and watches it bounce over the head of opposite number, Southampton's Artur Boruc, and into the net.

"It's a cool feeling but it was a fortunate incident. I feel a bit bad for Boruc."

Stoke's Asmir Begovic, the fifth goalkeeper to score in Premier League history.[9]

"I blame the wind."

And an embarrassed Artur Boruc[10]

Manchester City, meanwhile, restate their claim to the title with a crushing 7-0 win over Norwich, their biggest-ever win in the Premier League. In their next home game, against Spurs, they win 6-0 and embark on a 12-match unbeaten run where they win 11 games, including a 6-3 drubbing of league leaders Arsenal at the Etihad in December.

"What hurts most is we had an opportunity to have City nine points behind and now it's three. That is hard to swallow."

Arsène Wenger, Arsenal manager[11]

In the same month, Manchester United lose successive home games to Everton and Newcastle. It's the first time they've lost back-to-back league matches at Old Trafford since the 2001/2 season and leaves them ninth in the table, a colossal 13 points behind the pacesetters Arsenal.

There's better news down the M62 as Liverpool embark on their most serious title challenge in years. Brendan Rodgers' free-scoring side are top of the table at Christmas, having scored 20 goals in December, half of which have come from their Uruguayan striker Luis Suarez – the most ever by one player in a calendar month in the history of the Premier League.

> *"It was sheer brilliance. I always like to talk about the team but tonight you've got to hold up Luis as one of the best strikers in the world."*
>
> Brendan Rodgers sings the praises of Suarez after he nets four goals in a 5-1 win against Norwich City.[12]

After a Samuel Eto'o hat trick gives Chelsea a convincing 3-1 home win over Manchester United, the Blues welcome West Ham to Stamford Bridge, where Sam Allardyce's ultra-defensive strategy helps the Hammers to a goalless draw, putting paid to Chelsea's five-game winning streak.

"It's very difficult to play a football match where only one team wants to play, very difficult … I cannot be too critical because, if I was in this position, I don't know if I would do the same. But at the same time this is not Premier League. This is not the best league in the world. This is football from the 19th century."

A miffed Chelsea boss, José Mourinho…[13]

> "I don't give a s***e, to be honest. I love to see Chelsea players moaning at the referee, trying to intimidate the officials, and José jumping up and down in his technical area. It's great to see."
>
> And a delighted West Ham manager, Sam Allardyce.[14]

Despite a 1-0 away win at Manchester City that leaves Chelsea third in the table behind leaders Arsenal and Manchester City, manager José Mourinho maintains that his side still can't be considered as contenders for the Premier League crown.

> **"The title race is between two horses and a little horse that needs milk and needs to learn how to jump."**
>
> José Mourinho[15]

Soon after, Mourinho's arch enemy at Arsenal, Arsène Wenger, is asked why some of their fellow title challengers were so keen to rule themselves out of the title race.

"It is fear to fail."
Arsène Wenger[16]

Enter José Mourinho…

> **"He is a specialist in failure. I'm not. So if supposing he's right and I'm afraid of failure, it's because I don't fail many times. So maybe he's right. I'm not used to failing. But the reality is he's a specialist because, eight years without a piece of silverware, that's failure. If I did that in Chelsea I'd leave and not come back."**
>
> José Mourinho cuts Arsenal manager Arsène Wenger to the quick.[17]

There's a brouhaha at St James' Park where Newcastle's manager, Alan Pardew, tangles with Hull City's midfielder David Meyler as he tries to retrieve the ball for a throw-in. An unseemly scuffle ensues and ends with Pardew attempting to headbutt Meyler. It earns Pardew a £100,000 fine from his club, a three-game stadium ban, a further four games banned from the touchline and an additional £60,000 fine from the FA.

> **"We have held discussions with Alan, who has offered his sincere apologies. It is clear he deeply regrets his actions."**
>
> A statement from Newcastle United[18]

Meanwhile, it's Arsène Wenger's 100th game in charge at Arsenal as they visit Chelsea and leave having been humbled 6-0. The game is notable not just for the scoreline but for referee Andre Marriner sending off Arsenal's Kieran Gibbs when it's actually his teammate Alex Oxlade-Chamberlain that's the guilty party.

"Incidents of mistaken identity are very rare and are often the result of a number of different technical factors. Whilst this was a difficult decision Andre is disappointed that he failed to identify the correct player. He expressed his disappointment to Arsenal when he was made aware of the issue."

A statement from Professional Game Match Officials Limited[19]

It goes from bad to worse for David Moyes and Manchester United in March as they lose to their two fiercest rivals, Liverpool and Manchester City...

"We have played a very good side, playing at the sort of level we are aspiring to."

United manager David Moyes talks up Manchester City, after the Red Devils have been outclassed 3-0 at Old Trafford. Hardly the way to get an already sceptical following onside.[20]

"WRONG ONE – MOYES OUT"

A plane pulling a banner flies over Old Trafford, despite United's 4-1 win over Aston Villa.[21]

"I think the Manchester United fans who spent the money should have saved themselves a few quid: half of the ground didn't see it and the rest didn't pay very much attention to it."

BBC pundit Danny Mills[22]

David Moyes would have just two more games in charge of United, his final game a 2-0 defeat at his former club, Everton. On 22 April, Moyes was sacked, less than a year into his six-year contract. He's replaced by Ryan Giggs, who steps in to oversee the team's final four games of the season. When the season ends, United will go from being champions by 11 points to finishing in seventh place, their lowest placing since 1990. The Red Devils also fail to qualify for Europe for the first time in over 20 years.

"Moyes was the Badly Chosen One"

Headline in the *Manchester Evening News*[23]

With seven games to play, Chelsea's title aspirations wobble when they lose 2-1 to lowly Sunderland at Stamford Bridge. It's José Mourinho's first defeat in 77 league games as the Blues' boss and he's less than enamoured with referee Mike Dean, who awards the visitors a controversial late penalty.

"I want to congratulate again Mike Dean. I think his performance was unbelievable and I think when referees have unbelievable performances, I think it's fair that as managers we give them praise. So, fantastic performance."

José Mourinho's post-match sarcasm would earn him a £10,000 fine from the FA.[24]

There's a crunch game at Anfield in mid-April as leaders Liverpool face third-placed Manchester City. In an eventful match, Brendan Rodgers' side take a sizeable step towards their first top-flight title in 24 years by winning 3-2.

"They played like champions and in the next few weeks that is feasibly what they will be."

Daniel Taylor's match report in *The Guardian*[25]

Only they wouldn't.

On 27 April, and with the title in their hands, Liverpool host Chelsea at Anfield with the visitors also in with a chance of landing the trophy. But it would be a game that would go down in history for one moment and one moment alone. On the stroke of halftime, Steven Gerrard slips in possession, allowing Chelsea's Demba Ba to race away and score. When Willian adds a late second, it's a hammer blow to Liverpool's title hopes.

"And Gerrard slips! And Demba Ba is in here! Out comes Mignolet ... BA!"

Sky Sports commentator Martin Tyler on the moment it all started to unravel for Liverpool.[26]

Liverpool's 11-game winning run had come to a near-catastrophic ending and Steven Gerrard, the player that had so often been the man to rely on for the Reds, was the centre of attention again – for all the wrong reasons.

> "This is a boy who's picked up this club so many times, and it was just really unfortunate, at a crucial moment."
>
> Liverpool manager Brendan Rodgers[27]

In the match against Crystal Palace the following week, the Reds cruise into a three-goal lead but then concede three in the final 11 minutes to drop two more points. It's a collapse so dramatic that it has many Liverpool players in a state of shock at the final whistle.

"We're going to win the league."

Liverpool fans celebrate their side's third goal at Selhurst Park.[28]

> **"We got carried away. We thought we could score more."**
>
> Brendan Rodgers, blaming the capitulation on Liverpool's need to chase down Manchester City's superior goal difference.[29]

"For Liverpool the tears were flowing in the stands and on the pitch. They knew it was over."

The Guardian's Daniel Taylor.[30]

Liverpool's dramatic collapse left Manchester City effectively needing just four points from their final two games to win their second Premier League title in three seasons, thanks to their vastly superior goal difference. First they swept aside Aston Villa in style, beating them 4-0, then on the final day, they cantered to a 2-0 victory over West Ham at the Etihad Stadium. City were champions again.

"A beautiful great season."

Manuel Pellegrini, Manchester City's manager[31]

"You'll Never Win the League."

Manchester City fans adapt Liverpool's most famous song for their own purposes.[32]

It had been an intriguing and, at times, exceptional season. For the first time in the competition's history, two teams, Manchester City and Liverpool, had scored more than 100 goals. And it had been a brilliantly timed run from the eventual champions, too. Though the lead had changed a record 29 times over the course of the season, Manuel Pellegrini's team had only topped the table for 14 days in total. But they had scored 102 goals, just one short of Chelsea's all-time record, and an astonishing 61 goals at home in just 19 games.

But what of Steven Gerrard and that costly slip against Chelsea?

"There's not a day that goes by that I don't think about it hadn't happened. Would things have been different? ... Maybe, I don't know."

Steven Gerrard[33]

Games Played: 38

Pos	Team	GD	Pts
1	Manchester City	+65	86
2	Liverpool	+51	84
3	Chelsea	+44	82
4	Arsenal	+27	79
5	Everton	+22	72
6	Tottenham Hotspur	+4	69
7	Manchester United	+21	64
8	Southampton	+8	56
9	Stoke City	-7	50
10	Newcastle United	-16	49
11	Crystal Palace	-15	45
12	Swansea City	0	42
13	West Ham United	-11	40
14	Sunderland	-19	38
15	Aston Villa	-22	38
16	Hull City	-15	37
17	West Bromwich Albion	-16	36
18	Norwich City	-34	33
19	Fulham	-45	32
20	Cardiff City	-42	30

CHAMPIONS: Manchester City

RUNNERS-UP: Liverpool

RELEGATED: Norwich City, Fulham, Cardiff City

PROMOTED: Leicester City, Burnley, Queens Park Rangers

TOP GOALSCORER: Luis Suarez, Liverpool – 31

PLAYER OF THE SEASON: Luis Suarez, Liverpool

MANAGER OF THE SEASON: Tony Pulis, Stoke City

DID YOU KNOW? *A record number of managers – 10 – left their positions at Premier League clubs during the 2013/14 season.*

A Special Return

It was a summer where Germany became the first European side to win the World Cup in the Americas, beating Argentina 1-0 in Rio de Janeiro, Brazil, and, in the wake of the tournament, it had seemed as though England's Premier League clubs were intent on buying as many of the players from the event as was possible.

A total of £835 million was splurged in the summer transfer window. It's £200 million more than in the summer of 2013 and almost double the amount spent by the clubs in Spain's La Liga during the window.

Liverpool are very busy. They take the money from their £65 million sale of Luis Suarez to Barcelona and bring in a clutch of new signings to Anfield. They raid Southampton for Rickie Lambert (£4 million), Adam Lallana (£25 million) and Dejan Lovren (£20 million) and bring in Divock Origi (£10 million), Emre Can (£10 million), Lazar Markovic (£20 million) and Alberto Moreno (£12 million). But the signing that really grabs the headlines is the £16 million purchase of former Manchester City striker Mario Balotelli.

"I think we have done a really smart piece of business here. This transfer represents outstanding value for the club."

Liverpool manager Brendan Rodgers hails his £16 million new signing, Mario Balotelli. The Italian will go on to score just four goals in 28 games for the Reds before being sent out on loan to AC Milan.[1]

Just as in the previous season, all eyes are on Manchester United as their new manager, the Dutchman Louis van Gaal, takes over at Old Trafford. With a CV that stands comparison with the best managers in the game, he arrives at United charged with restoring the team to the glories of the Ferguson era. Like Liverpool, United go big in the transfer market, spending over £165 million on new players, including Ander Herrera, Luke Shaw, Marcos Rojo,

Radamel Falcao, Daley Blind and the new £59.7 million British record signing, Argentina's Angel Di Maria.

But it doesn't go to plan. United lose their first game of the season at home to Swansea City and win just three of their first 10 games – their worst ever start in the Premier League.

> **"Believe me, Manchester United, the manager of Manchester United and all the players and staff want to win every game and we do everything to win the game every week."**
>
> Louis van Gaal, Manchester United manager[2]

A key defeat, meanwhile, comes at Leicester City's King Power Stadium, where United surrender a 3-1 lead and lose 5-3 in spectacular fashion.

> *"It is not good because we had the game in our pocket and gave it away. Not because of Leicester; we gave it away and I don't like that."*
>
> United's unhappy manager, Louis van Gaal[3]

"It's not been an easy journey to come here, and now we are at the top, but it's all about staying here now."

Leicester manager Nigel Pearson, after a win that took his side to seventh place, not top.[4]

Bolstered by the signings of Arsenal's Cesc Fabregas, Atletico Madrid striker Diego Costa and the return of Didier Drogba on a one-year contract, Chelsea begin the campaign in imperious form, winning seven of their first eight matches.

> "If you bring him back it is not because he is Didier or scored the most important goal in the history of Chelsea, or because I read I need an assistant, no. We want to win matches and win titles and Didier is one of the best strikers in Europe."
>
> José Mourinho, Chelsea manager[5]

The only blip in an otherwise faultless start was a 1-1 draw with Manchester City, where their legendary midfielder Frank Lampard, now on loan at City, scored a late equaliser to snatch a draw for the Etihad club. It's a goal that almost brings Lampard to tears.

> **"It's a tough one for me. I had 13 amazing years with the Chelsea fans, so I am mixed with it ... I am a little lost for words..."**
>
> Frank Lampard[6]

Not that Chelsea manager José Mourinho has any room for sentiment...

"He is a Man City player. I don't believe in these histories of passion and heart, I don't believe in these. Maybe I am too pragmatic in football. When he decided to come to Man City, a direct competitor of Chelsea, love stories are over."[7]

The long-running feud between José Mourinho and Arsène Wenger boils over as Chelsea defeat Arsenal 2-0 at Stamford Bridge. Twenty minutes into the game, the Blues' defender Gary Cahill is booked for a bad tackle on Alexis Sanchez but the Arsenal manager is furious that it's not a red card, making his point by shoving Mourinho on the touchline.

"In hindsight I think I should not have reacted at all, it's not a way to behave on a football field. I always regret any signs of violence and I apologise, but that's a part of games where everything is manic."

Arsène Wenger, Arsenal manager[8]

> **"Charged? If it was me, it would have been a stadium ban."**
>
> Chelsea boss José Mourinho responds to suggestions that Wenger could be charged for his conduct.[9]

At White Hart Lane in October, there's the fastest ever goal by a Premier League substitute when Newcastle's Sammy Ameobi comes on at halftime and scores just eight seconds after the restart.

"A stupid goal."

Mauricio Pochettino, Spurs manager[10]

Leicester City's 3-1 home defeat to Liverpool, meanwhile, is overshadowed by a row between Foxes' boss Nigel Pearson and a Leicester fan in the stands. He is found guilty of using abusive language towards a spectator, fined £10,000 and given a one-match touchline ban for his conduct.

> *"I've had run-ins with fans in the past and in the heat of the moment these things happen. I'm not going to repeat what happened on either side. I'm more than happy to stand up for myself in that situation. If people were offended then that is regrettable. But there is no need to apologise to somebody of that ilk."*

Nigel Pearson, Leicester manager[11]

As Leicester's faltering form sees their Premier League status hanging in the balance, the pressure gets to manager Nigel Pearson. Again. During a 1-0 home defeat to Crystal Palace, he grapples with the Eagles' midfielder James McArthur on the touchline, grabbing him by the throat and then refusing to let him go.

"I'm more than capable of looking after myself."

Leicester boss Nigel Pearson[12]

By New Year's Day, it's clear that Chelsea's chief challengers in the title race will be the defending champions, Manchester City. A 3-2 victory over Sunderland puts Manuel Pellegrini's side level on points, goal difference and goals scored with Chelsea, who lose 5-3 to Spurs at White Hart Lane. It's only the second time in his 14-year managerial career that a side of José Mourinho's has conceded five goals in a game.

"We trust our game but maybe it's not enough."

José Mourinho, Chelsea manager[13]

After a 3-1 home defeat to Chelsea ends a run of four consecutive wins for Leicester, manager Nigel Pearson, no stranger to controversy, snaps in a press conference and goes for reporter Ian Baker.

"If you don't know the answer to that question, then I think you are an ostrich. Are you flexible enough to get your head in the sand? My suspicion would be no. I can. You can't."

Nigel Pearson, Leicester manager[14]

There's trouble too for Newcastle where, after eight defeats in a row send the Magpies plummeting down the league table, manager John Carver is forced to defend his credentials.

"I still think I'm the best coach in the Premier League."

John Carver, Newcastle manager. He is sacked in the summer, having won just three games in five months.[15]

History is made in the penultimate round of fixtures as Southampton's Senegalese striker Sadio Mane scores the fastest Premier League hat trick ever, rifling home three goals against Aston Villa in just 2 minutes and 56 seconds. The feat eclipses the record held by Liverpool's Robbie Fowler by over a minute and a half.

"In Senegal they will be happy for me ... I am happy."

Southampton's Sadio Mane[16]

Mane's hat trick is the icing on the cake for Saints as they finish the season in seventh, their highest ever placing, with a league-high total of 60 points. It's testament to the work of their Dutch coach Ronald Koeman and comes despite losing five key players in the transfer window.

"Others at the club deserve credit too but Koeman's opening season in English football has been nothing short of sensational, not just matching Mauricio Pochettino's win percentage, but blowing it to pieces."

Colin Murray, *The Metro*[17]

The final day and after a career spanning 17 years at Liverpool, their inspirational captain Steven Gerrard plays his last game for the club away at Stoke City. While he scores, it's hardly the send-off he deserves as the Reds return home on the back of a 6-1 mauling. It's also a game that sees former Liverpool striker Peter Crouch break Alan Shearer's record for headed goals in the Premier League with his 47th in the competition.

> "All supporters connected with Liverpool will be embarrassed by that and deserve an apology. The first half was awful. Absolutely awful. I have always said if the owners want me to go I go it is as simple as that. But I still feel I have a lot to offer here."
>
> Liverpool manager Brendan Rodgers and what would be the beginning of the end of his tenure at Anfield.[18]

"I started supporting the club at a very young age. A lot of my family are Reds. The way the club shaped me and treated me from a very young age and turned me into a decent human being and a good footballer – I've got a lot to thank them for."

Liverpool legend Steven Gerrard on what the club means to him.[19]

Liverpool finish the season in sixth place, eight points adrift of the Champions League places. Worryingly, they score just 52 goals, almost half the number they scored in 2013/14 and exactly the same number that Luis Suarez and Daniel Sturridge scored between them that season.

It's also the end of the Premier League road for Frank Lampard as he plays his final game for Manchester City. Fittingly, he scores in a 2-0 win.

> *"It was emotional. My last ever game in the Premier League and I didn't realise my daughters would be on the pitch. People can talk about whether this was the right decision for me or not. This was completely the right decision – I've lost nothing from what I did at Chelsea."*
>
> Frank Lampard after the last of his 609 appearances in the Premier League.[20]

As Sunderland avoid the drop yet again, their Dutch manager Dick Advocaat decides that his marriage is more important than spending another season at the Stadium of Light.

"No, no, no, I'll get a divorce."

Black Cats' boss Dick Advocaat, who did decide to stay, after all. He is still married.[21]

Remarkably, Leicester City also survive, despite occupying the bottom spot in the table for 140 days of the season. It's the longest spell at the foot of the league that any team has spent and not been relegated, but they win seven of their last nine league games to pull off the greatest of escapes.

> *"Let's keep the celebrations in context. It's a fabulous achievement but I wouldn't want to be looking at avoiding relegation as a target to aspire to."*
>
> Leicester boss Nigel Pearson after his side beat QPR 5-1 on the final day, condemning the west London team to bottom spot in the Premier League and relegation.[22]

The season would also see Burnley and Hull City relegated.

But it's Chelsea's title again. They top the table for a record 274 days in the season and win their fourth Premier League title with three games to spare, a 1-0 home win over Crystal Palace taking them over the line.

"Unbelievable. We've worked so hard to get there. It was a little bit nervy but we've done it. One person said I couldn't play two times in a week. Who knows who he is? I've proved him wrong. I've been ballboy here, I've been mascot, I've painted the stadium."

Chelsea captain John Terry, who became only the second outfield player (after Gary Pallister in 1992/3) to play every minute for a Premier League title-winning team.[23]

> **"We did everything the team needs to do. That's why we're champions. That's why we deserve it. Everybody knows that. The people who have a big face to say we don't deserve it are the ones who, in my country, we have a saying for: the dogs bark and the caravan goes by."**
>
> José Mourinho, Manager of the Year. Your guess is as good as ours.[24]

Games Played: 38

Pos	Team	GD	Pts
1	Chelsea	+41	87
2	Manchester City	+45	79
3	Arsenal	+35	75
4	Manchester United	+25	70
5	Tottenham Hotspur	+5	64
6	Liverpool	+4	62
7	Southampton	+21	60
8	Swansea City	-3	56
9	Stoke City	+3	54
10	Crystal Palace	-4	48
11	Everton	-2	47
12	West Ham United	-3	47
13	West Bromwich Albion	-13	44
14	Leicester City	-9	41
15	Newcastle United	-23	39
16	Sunderland	-22	38
17	Aston Villa	-26	38
18	Hull City	-18	35
19	Burnley	-25	33
20	Queens Park Rangers	-31	30

CHAMPIONS: Chelsea

RUNNERS-UP: Manchester City

RELEGATED: QPR, Burnley, Hull City

PROMOTED: Watford, AFC Bournemouth, Norwich City

TOP GOALSCORER: Sergio Aguero, Manchester City – 26

PLAYER OF THE SEASON: Eden Hazard, Chelsea

MANAGER OF THE SEASON: José Mourinho, Chelsea

DID YOU KNOW? *Everton's Gareth Barry became the first player to receive 100 yellow cards in the Premier League when he was booked against Stoke on Boxing Day 2014.*

PREMIER LEAGUE 2015/16

5000 to One

In the history of the Premier League there had only ever been five winners of England's most coveted title. Manchester United, of course, had dominated the event, taking 13 crowns, followed by Chelsea (4), Arsenal (3), Manchester City (2) and Blackburn Rovers (1).

But there would be a new name on the trophy in 2015/16 – and it was a name that nobody, not in their wildest, most absurd dreams, could ever have imagined.

It's a summer of change. West Ham replace Sam Allardyce with the Croat Slaven Bilic, Watford bring in the Spaniard Quique Sanchez Flores, Newcastle hire Steve McClaren, and Leicester, after their brush with relegation, appoint the former Chelsea coach Claudio Ranieri as their new manager.

The 63-year-old Italian arrives at the King Power Stadium after a disastrous four-month spell as manager of the Greek national team, a reign that comes to an end the morning after a humiliating defeat to the Faroe Islands.

It's an appointment that's met with widespread indifference.

"Claudio Ranieri? Really?"

Underwhelmed *Match of the Day* presenter and lifelong Leicester fan Gary Lineker takes to Twitter.[1]

"If Leicester wanted someone nice, they've got him. If they wanted someone to keep them in the Premier League, then they may have gone for the wrong guy."

Marcus Christenson, *The Guardian*[2]

There's trouble at Ranieri's former employers on the opening day of the season. With time running out in their home game against Swansea, their star man, Eden Hazard, is tripped and goes down injured. As Chelsea are already down to 10 men, manager José Mourinho is infuriated when his medical team, Eva Carneiro and Jon Fearn, run on to the pitch to treat the Belgian, potentially leaving Chelsea with just nine men to hang on for a 2-2 draw.

> **"I was unhappy with my medical staff. They were impulsive and naive. Whether you are a kit man, doctor or secretary on the bench you have to understand the game. You have to know you have one player less and to assist a player you must be sure he has a serious problem. I was sure Eden did not have a serious problem. He had a knock. He was tired."**
>
> José Mourinho, Chelsea manager[3]

A little over a month later, the never-ending feud between José Mourinho and Arsène Wenger is resumed as Chelsea beat the Gunners 2-0 at Stamford Bridge, with Arsenal reduced to just nine men after red cards for Gabriel and Santi Cazorla. The villain of the piece is Chelsea striker Diego Costa, whom Wenger blames for provoking his players.

> "He [Costa] will do the same again next week and the week after and he always gets away with it."
>
> Arsène Wenger, Arsenal manager[4]

> **"If you want to speak about Diego Costa with me, he played like he has to play. That's why you have full stadiums and you sell to televisions around the world for millions and millions, because the game has to be played like that…"**
>
> José Mourinho, Chelsea manager[5]

Manchester City's prolific striker Sergio Aguero becomes only the fifth player in Premier League history to score five goals in a game when he helps himself in a 6-1 win in early October. The five-goal haul comes in just 20 minutes and Aguero is taken off after 66 minutes. In the return fixture in May, Aguero would score again, his 100th in the division. He reaches the century in just 147 games. Indeed, only Alan Shearer has reached the milestone quicker (124 games).

The following day, after three and a half years at the club, Liverpool dismiss manager Brendan Rodgers in the wake of a 1-1 draw with neighbours Everton. With just four wins from 11 games in all competitions, the club's owners, Fenway Sports Group, decide that a change of manager is needed and, four days later, appoint the German coach Jurgen Klopp.

"Rodgers can't argue in some ways. He's been there three years, he hasn't won a trophy and they've played Champions League football once. That's not good enough for Liverpool. Liverpool are becoming Tottenham."

Former Liverpool defender Jamie Carragher.[6]

....

Charismatic and forward-thinking, the 48-year-old had guided unfashionable Borussia Dortmund to back-to-back Bundesliga titles and taken them to the final of the 2013 Champions League. Now, he was charged with bringing the glory days back to Anfield. He wastes no time in charming the media.

"I am not going to call myself anything. I am a normal guy from the Black Forest. My mother is watching this press conference at home. If you are going to call me anything, call me the Normal One. I was a very average player and became a trainer in Germany with a special club."

Echoes of José Mourinho as Jurgen Klopp holds his first press conference as Liverpool manager.[7]

....

Determined to shore up his defence, Leicester manager Claudio Ranieri reveals his new tactic to help his back line as they concede in each of the first nine games of the season. It works too, as they shut out Crystal Palace in a 1-0 win.

"I told them, the clean sheet, I buy everybody a pizza. I think they wait until I improve my offer, okay a pizza and a hot dog."

Claudio Ranieri[8]

History is made on 21 November when Leicester City striker Jamie Vardy scores in his 11th consecutive Premier League game. It's a new record and eclipses the 10-game streak held by Vardy and former Manchester United striker Ruud Van Nistelrooy.

"Obviously, cheers boys. I wouldn't have been able to do it without you all. The gaffer's just said he's going to put some beers on the coach and the plane."

Jamie Vardy reveals plans for a celebratory knees-up.[9]

As Chelsea's form suffers in the fallout of the Eva Carneiro affair, the Blues suffer a 2-1 defeat at Leicester City and manager José Mourinho isn't happy…

"I feel like my work was betrayed."

José Mourinho[10]

The Leicester game will be José Mourinho's last in charge at Stamford Bridge. Lying one place above the relegation zone and having lost nine of their 16 league games, Mourinho is removed from his position on 17 December, with Guus Hiddink returning for a second spell as caretaker manager. It's just seven months since Chelsea were crowned champions of England and four months since the Portuguese signed a new four-year, £13 million-a-year contract.

"The club wishes to make clear José leaves us on good terms and will always remain a much-loved, respected and significant figure at Chelsea … The club's focus is now on ensuring our talented squad reaches its potential."

Chelsea club statement[11]

"It has imploded in front of our eyes. It is astonishing. I saw players who were not giving everything. There is no trust there, respect is gone. Ultimately it is easier to change a manager than 22 players."

Martin Keown, former Arsenal and England defender.[12]

The victory for Leicester, meanwhile, sees the Foxes top the Premier League table going into Christmas. It's a turnaround in their fortunes that nobody predicted back in August.

"From the beginning when something was wrong I've been saying: 'Dilly-ding, dilly-dong, wake up, wake up!' So on Christmas Day I bought for all the players and all the staff a little bell. It was just a joke."

Claudio Ranieri, Leicester manager[13]

> "YES! If Leicester win the @premierleague I'll do the first MOTD of next season in just my undies."
>
> Gary Lineker and the tweet he'll come to regret.[14]

Along with the goals of Harry Kane, Spurs' title challenge is given real impetus by the performances of 19-year-old Dele Alli. A £5 million buy from Milton Keynes, he scores five goals and makes three goals in his first 18 league games and is rewarded with a new long-term contract in mid-January. Soon after, he scores the Goal of the Season at Crystal Palace, flicking up the ball on the edge of the area, spinning round and volleying home.

> **"Well, I've seen some glorious goals scored in my time watching football matches but I doubt whether I will see a goal scored with such individual flair, and by a 19-year-old … it was sheer class."**
>
> Garth Crooks, former Spurs striker and football pundit.[15]

Despite a mediocre season by Manchester United's stratospherically high standards, there is at least a glimmer of hope for the future as a new talent emerges. When United play Arsenal at Old Trafford in February, teenage striker Marcus Rashford makes a dream debut, scoring twice and setting up the winner for Ander Herrera in a 3-2 victory. Coincidentally, he is exactly the same age (18 years and 120 days) as Wayne Rooney was when he scored his first double for United.

> **"It's crazy. You can't explain it. It's a rush."**
>
> Marcus Rashford, United's new hero.[16]

Bournemouth record back-to-back wins at Chelsea and, a week later, at home to Manchester United. It's the first time a newly promoted team have beaten the reigning champions since Bolton's win at Old Trafford in 2001/2.

"In my opinion it's probably the biggest result in the club's history."

Bournemouth manager Eddie Howe beams after the win at Stamford Bridge. The Cherries would enjoy a successful debut in the top flight, finishing 16th.[17]

After just six victories in 28 Premier League victories and with the club just one place off the foot of the table, Newcastle sack their manager Steve McClaren. He is replaced by Rafa Benitez, the man who steered Liverpool to Champions League glory in 2005.

"I have the pleasure to confirm I have committed to a legendary English club … C'mon Toon Army! The club and I need your total involvement!"

Rafa Benitez announces his arrival on Tyneside via a club statement. The Spaniard fails to keep the Magpies in the top flight, however, as they end the season in 18th place.[18]

The defeat to Bournemouth is the start of a three-match losing streak for United, with losses against Norwich and Stoke coming amid reports that the former Chelsea manager José Mourinho is being lined up to take over at Old Trafford. When Louis van Gaal meets the press soon after, he's not best pleased.

"Has anybody in this room got a feeling to apologise to me? That's what I am wondering. I think I was already sacked … do you think I want to talk with the media now? I am here only because of the Premier League rules. I have to talk with you. Merry Christmas. Enjoy the wine and a mince pie. Goodbye."

Louis van Gaal, Manchester United manager[19]

Leicester's title celebrations are put on hold in early May as they play out a fiery encounter with Manchester United at Old Trafford. There's a red card for the Foxes' Danny Drinkwater, and Marouane Fellaini and Robert Huth are both banned for three matches as the Foxes' defender pulls Fellaini's hair and the United man responds by elbowing him in the face. The game ends 1-1.

> ### "It's not in the books that somebody has to grab with the hair and pull from behind. Only in sex masochism, then it is allowed."
> United manager Louis van Gaal gives his verdict on the fracas.[20]

"It is important to finish the story like an American movie. Always in the end it is OK. There is a happy ending."

Claudio Ranieri, keen to complete the miracle.[21]

After 112 years at the Boleyn Ground, West Ham prepare for their move to the London Stadium and bid farewell to their east London home in a pulsating game against Manchester United. The Hammers come from behind to win 3-2 with a late winner from Winston Reid.

> ### "I think it was written in the stars tonight."
> Mark Noble, West Ham skipper and lifelong Hammers fan.[22]

"It was just meant to be. It was one of those evenings for us, a special occasion for the whole club."

Winston Reid, West Ham's match-winner[23]

> ### *"The stadium deserves this kind of farewell."*
> West Ham manager Slaven Bilic. His team would finish in seventh place with 62 points, a Premier League record for the club.[24]

Meanwhile, Leicester City finally claim the title when they're not even playing. The Foxes' squad assemble at Jamie Vardy's house and watch closest challengers Spurs draw 2-2 at Chelsea on television. It's a result that, remarkably, confirms Leicester as the Premier League champions for 2015/16.

> **"It's mental what has happened. Someone must have put a spell on me to make this season happen."**
>
> Leicester's striker Jamie Vardy[25]

Having narrowly avoided relegation in 2014/15, Leicester had gone into the season as 5000-1 outsiders to win the Premier League title and now, nine miraculous months later, they had not only avoided the drop but won the Premier League title by 10 points.

> **"I'm emotionally drained. It's an unbelievable feeling to finally get my hands on the trophy. Walking up to the podium I got emotional, I had to hold back tears. I held them back and finally got my hands on it, lifted it and it's the best feeling in the world."**
>
> Wes Morgan, Leicester captain[26]

> **"I always thought I'd be a champion ... but I didn't think it would be here."**
>
> Claudio Ranieri, Leicester City manager[27]

Games Played: 38

Pos	Team	GD	Pts
1	Leicester City	+32	81
2	Arsenal	+29	71
3	Tottenham Hotspur	+34	70
4	Manchester City	+30	66
5	Manchester United	+14	66
6	Southampton	+18	63
7	West Ham United	+14	62
8	Liverpool	+13	60
9	Stoke City	-14	51
10	Chelsea	+6	50
11	Everton	+4	47
12	Swansea City	-10	47
13	Watford	-10	45
14	West Bromwich Albion	-14	43
15	Crystal Palace	-12	42
16	AFC Bournemouth	-22	42
17	Sunderland	-14	39
18	Newcastle United	-21	37
19	Norwich City	-28	34
20	Aston Villa	-49	17

CHAMPIONS: Leicester City

RUNNERS-UP: Arsenal

RELEGATED: Newcastle United, Norwich City, Aston Villa

PROMOTED: Burnley, Hull City, Middlesbrough

TOP GOALSCORER: Harry Kane, Tottenham Hotspur – 25

PLAYER OF THE SEASON: Jamie Vardy, Leicester City

MANAGER OF THE SEASON: Claudio Ranieri, Leicester City

DID YOU KNOW? *This year was the first time in Premier League history that the opening goal of the season was an own goal. Kyle Walker of Spurs was the unlucky player, putting through his own net against Manchester United.*

PREMIER LEAGUE 2016/17

The Blues Roar Back

The 25th season of the Premier League saw the competition's new sponsorless rebrand come into being. No brewer, no finance company, no nothing. From now on, it would be simply 'The Premier League', complete with an eye-catching new lion logo. There's good news for fans too, as, for the first time, match tickets for travelling fans are capped at £30.

The close season sees a glut of managerial changes with some heavyweight names arriving in the Premier League. Some, like Antonio Conte and Pep Guardiola, make their debut in the division while others, like José Mourinho, return for another try.

Conte arrives at Chelsea having guided Italy to the quarter-finals of the European Championships and, prior to that, led Juventus to a hat trick of Serie A titles.

> **"I hope that, during the season, I'll leave you this opportunity to find a new name for me. I hope to be a good name, not a bad name."**
>
> Antonio Conte's response when asked if he was the new 'Special One'.[1]

On 27 May, Manchester United confirm the worst-kept secret in football when they appoint the former Chelsea manager José Mourinho to take over from Louis van Gaal at Old Trafford.

> **"To become Manchester United manager is a special honour in the game. It is a club known and admired throughout the world. There is a mystique and a romance about it which no other club can match."**
>
> José Mourinho, new Manchester United manager[2]

On the other side of Manchester, there's another heavyweight manager arriving in town as Pep Guardiola finally takes over at City. The former Barcelona and Bayern Munich coach had been announced as the successor to Manuel Pellegrini in February but now, on 1 July, had finally taken the reins at the Etihad.

> **"Good morning to everybody, it's our first time here. Fasten your seat belt for the other side of the car. I just arrived 10 days ago, we are here still knowing each other so I need time. But we are going to try to do our best for our people, especially for our players to be happy with what they do. And obviously for our fans, at the end to try and be proud."**
>
> Pep Guardiola introduces himself at his first Manchester City press conference.[3]

Meanwhile, Everton pinch Ronald Koeman from Southampton and the Saints replace him with the Frenchman Claude Puel. Watford appoint Walter Mazzarri, Hull City give Mike Phelan a chance and David Moyes returns to the Premier League, replacing the new England manager Sam Allardyce as boss of Sunderland.

There's a clutch of high-profile signings on the pitch, too. After a lacklustre defence of their title, Chelsea bolster their ranks with N'Golo Kanté, Michy Batshuayi, Marcos Alonso and, in a shock return to Stamford Bridge, defender David Luiz.

Manchester City, meanwhile, waste no time in giving Pep Guardiola what he wants, signing Ilkay Gündogan, Nolito and Everton's John Stones. Controversially, Guardiola also lures the Barcelona keeper Claudio Bravo to City, allowing their England number one, Joe Hart, to move on loan to Italian club Torino.

"Claudio is a fantastic goalkeeper and an excellent addition to our squad. He has experience and great leadership qualities and is in the prime of his life. He is a goalkeeper I have admired for a number of years and I'm really happy he is now a City player."
Pep Guardiola[4]

But neighbours Manchester United up the ante still further. Not only do they sign Henrikh Mkhitaryan and the Swedish superstar Zlatan Ibrahimovic but they smash the world record for a transfer fee to buy Juventus midfielder Paul Pogba, a player the Red Devils had let go for just £1.5 million four years earlier.

"I feel the time is right to go back to Old Trafford. I always enjoyed playing in front of the fans and can't wait to make my contribution to the team. This is the right club for me to achieve everything I hope to in the game."

The most expensive player in the world, Paul Pogba.[5]

The season begins on 13 August and Manchester United's new superstar signing Zlatan Ibrahimovic marks his league debut with a 25-yard goal in a 3–1 win against Bournemouth.

A week later, West Ham play their first league game at the newly named London Stadium, winning 1–0 against Bournemouth. But it's not the smoothest of moves as crowd trouble, a lack of atmosphere and the distance of the stands from the pitch all prompt complaints.

"It doesn't feel like a home game, it can't feel like that. But it's not an away game also, it's a home game because we are home, we are in London and we're going to a Canary Wharf hotel for a meal and all that."

Slaven Bilic, West Ham manager[6]

Just two games into the season and with Sunderland having lost both of their matches, new manager David Moyes admits that his club are in real danger of relegation again.

> *"Well, they would probably be right. That's where they've been every other year for the last four years, so why would it suddenly change? I think it will be, I don't think you can hide the facts, that will be the case, yes. People will be flat because they are hoping that something is going to dramatically change – it can't dramatically change, it can't."*
>
> David Moyes responds to suggestions that Sunderland's fans are fearing another battle against relegation.[7]

There are no such problems for Manchester City. Under new manager Pep Guardiola, the Citizens win their first six league games (as part of a 10-match winning streak) before a 2–0 defeat at Spurs finally brings their run to an end.

Part of the run sees arch-enemies José Mourinho and Pep Guardiola reunited as United and City clash at Old Trafford, and while City emerge as 2–1 winners, the game is noticeable for a debut clanger from new keeper Claudio Bravo that allows Zlatan Ibrahimovic to score.

"Claudio Bravo may not be great at catching crosses but he's great with his feet."

Gary Lineker takes to Twitter.[8]

As does Ian Wright…

"Claudio Bravo is terrible."

After three wins in their first four games, Chelsea suffer consecutive losses to Liverpool and Arsenal and the nature of the defeats prompts manager Antonio Conte to change his formation. He switches to a back three and it proves to be an inspired decision as the Blues go on a 13-match winning streak.

> **"I'm happy I did because, now, we are top of the league and, back then, we were eight points behind Manchester City. That just shows the situation can change very quickly."**
>
> Antonio Conte, Chelsea manager[9]

The Blues' 2–1 home defeat to Liverpool comes after a stunning goal from their skipper Jordan Henderson, who curls a long-range effort into the top corner from 28 yards, capping a fine performance from Jurgen Klopp's side.

> **"We played football like hell."**
>
> Jurgen Klopp, Liverpool manager[10]

Across London at the Emirates, it's the 20th anniversary of Arsène Wenger's arrival at Arsenal. Two decades on and the Frenchman is the longest-serving manager in British football.

> **"It's a great honour, 20 years. It shows total commitment from the club and faith in me through good times and less good times, it is a great privilege especially in my job to last such a long time. It is a great honour."**
>
> Arsène Wenger, Chelsea manager[11]

It's a less impressive start for the reigning champions, Leicester City. They lose six of their first 12 games, winning just three.

> *"Our position is not good, but with this spirit I am calm and confident with my players. It's a bad period now but we have to react and keep going. We must stay strong."*
>
> Leicester's beleaguered manager Claudio Ranieri after a 2–1 defeat away at Watford.[12]

A mere 11 games into his tenure at the Liberty Stadium, Swansea decide to part company with their American manager Bob Bradley. He is replaced by the former Real Madrid and Bayern Munich assistant, Paul Clement.

"I'm a little bit pissed off ... I don't think it's the correct decision."

A disgruntled Bob Bradley.[13]

Having been sacked as England manager after just 67 days in charge of the national team, Sam Allardyce makes a swift return to club management as he takes the reins at struggling Crystal Palace.

"Let's stop losing."

Sam Allardyce's rallying cry at his first press conference as Crystal Palace manager. The great escape specialist will guide the Eagles to safety, ending the season in 14th place.[14]

Chelsea's fine winning run finally comes to an end in the Blues' first fixture of the new year as they lose 2–0 at Spurs, with both goals coming from the head of Dele Alli.

"It is one step forward for the team and is important to keep going. Football is about belief."

Mauricio Pochettino, Tottenham manager[15]

There are two extraordinary goals within a week as Manchester United's Henrikh Mkhitaryan and Arsenal's Olivier Giroud both score what become known as 'scorpion kick' goals, throwing out their leg behind them and back-heeling the ball over their heads and into the goal.

"Oli's goal was very lucky. He can try that 10 times but I am not sure he would score it 10 times. He had a little bit of luck for that goal but he tried it, so it is a nice goal."

Giroud's skipper, Laurent Koscielny[16]

But they would be outdone by a wonder goal from West Ham's Andy Carroll, who scores the most spectacular overhead scissor kick against Crystal Palace.

> *"It's been a while in the making – I've been trying for a couple of years. It's got to be the best goal I've scored."*
>
> Andy Carroll[17]

"With his history of injuries I go a bit crazy when he does that in training because you don't want him to get hurt."

Slaven Bilic, West Ham manager[18]

January is also the month where Wayne Rooney becomes Manchester United's all-time leading goalscorer, his brilliant stoppage time goal salvaging a point against Stoke City and taking him to 250 goals, one ahead of Sir Bobby Charlton.

> "I'm disappointed in not getting three points, but there is no denying that it's a proud moment for me and a huge honour to get that record. Just a bit dampened, if you like, by the result."
>
> Manchester United's new record goalscorer, Wayne Rooney.[19]

On 23 February, just nine months after leading Leicester City to the most miraculous title win in Premier League history, Claudio Ranieri is sacked by the club. The Foxes have lost five games in a row, lie just one point above the relegation zone and have yet to score a league goal in 2017.

"This has been the most difficult decision we have had to make in nearly seven years since King Power took ownership of Leicester City, but we are duty-bound to put the club's long-term interests above all sense of personal sentiment, no matter how strong that might be."

Aiyawatt Srivaddhanaprabha, Leicester vice-chairman[20]

"Yesterday, my dream died. After the euphoria of last season and being crowned Premier League champions, all I dreamt of was staying with Leicester City, the club I love, for always. Sadly this was not to be. My heartfelt thanks to everybody at the club, all the players, the staff, everybody who was there and was part of what we achieved. But mostly to the supporters. You took me into your hearts from day one and loved me. I love you, too. No one can ever take away what we together have achieved, and I hope you think about it and smile every day the way I always will."

An emotional Claudio Ranieri.[21]

"After all that Claudio Ranieri has done for Leicester City, to sack him now is inexplicable, unforgivable and gut-wrenchingly sad."

Leicester legend Gary Lineker takes to Twitter.[22]

There are changes afoot on Teesside too, where, despite him leading Middlesbrough into the Premier League, club chairman Steve Gibson calls time on manager Aitor Karanka's time at the Riverside. Boro are languishing in the relegation zone without a win in 10 league games and have scored just 19 goals all season. Assistant head coach Steve Agnew is given the job on an interim basis.

"This club will always hold a special place for me."

Aitor Karanka[23]

As Arsenal travel to West Bromwich Albion, the ongoing debate about whether their manager, Arsène Wenger, should remain in his job takes to the skies above Britain's highest football ground. Two planes fly over the ground, one carrying a pro-Wenger banner…

"IN ARSENE WE TRUST. #RESPECTAW"

The other demanding he goes…

"NO CONTRACT #WENGER OUT"

There's an ill-tempered encounter at Old Trafford as Manchester United and Bournemouth play out a 1–1 draw. Towards the end of the first half, the Cherries' defender Tyrone Mings appears to stamp on the head of the prostrate Zlatan Ibrahimovic and the Swede responds by elbowing Mings in the face.

"Unluckily he jumped into my elbow."
Zlatan Ibrahimovic's interpretation of the incident.[24]

Both men are later charged with violent conduct. Ibrahimovic is given a three-game ban while Mings receives a five-match ban.

"For people to deem that I could intentionally stamp on a fellow professional's head is upsetting. It is an action that would not be acceptable in any walk of life, let alone on a football pitch, and one that would never cross my mind."
Tyrone Mings' Twitter response to his ban.[25]

Ever the football coach, Chelsea manager Antonio Conte returns home to see his family in Italy – and then goes to watch his old team, Juventus.

"When I told my wife I was going to watch Juventus she wasn't happy. She said, 'Why? Stay with us – your daughter and your wife.' But sometimes it's not easy to explain to my wife my choice when I have a day off."

Antonio Conte, Chelsea manager[26]

As Manchester United face a glut of matches in April, José Mourinho continues with his seemingly never-ending moan about the plight of his side.

"It is not human."

José Mourinho, Manchester United manager[27]

But it's wearing thin with many in the game.

"If you are Manchester United manager, I think you want to play nine games in April, because it shows you are still in competitions, still going for things … I don't see anything out of the ordinary in the number of games they have played. This year they could play 63 games, last year they played 59 so not a massive difference."

Sky Sports pundit Jamie Carragher[28]

Meanwhile, as United host struggling Swansea at Old Trafford there's outrage as their teenage England striker Marcus Rashford clearly dives to win a penalty. The game ends 1–1.

"My initial thought at the time, seeing how my players reacted to it, was that they clearly thought it wasn't. I've seen the replay and the player has deceived the referee. It's clear, there's no other way to look at it."

Paul Clement, Swansea City manager[29]

As Liverpool try to cement a top four finish and a place in the Champions League, they have the German midfielder Emre Can to thank for a goal of the season contender that wins the match against Watford.

> **"You don't expect him to do that. It's sublime. That is perfect, no shinning, straight in off the foot."**
>
> Sky Sports pundit Alan Pardew[30]

After back-to-back 3–0 wins against Everton and Middlesbrough, Chelsea travelled to The Hawthorns knowing that victory over West Bromwich Albion would secure them their fifth Premier League title. Though Tony Pulis' side hold out for 82 minutes, they are finally beaten by a goal from the substitute Michy Batshuayi, who slides the ball home from close range to win the title for Chelsea.

Meanwhile, Antonio Conte becomes the fourth Italian manager to win the English top-flight title, after Carlo Ancelotti, Roberto Mancini and Claudio Ranieri. He has transformed the Chelsea team from an inconsistent mid-table side to worthy champions and all in less than a year.

> **"It's a great achievement for the players. I have to give thanks for their commitment and work-rate and patience, they showed me great attitude and great desire to try to do something great in the season... It wasn't easy for me to arrive in England to try a different habit, a different language and also a lot of players after a bad season."**
>
> Antonio Conte, Chelsea manager[31]

"He works with passion every day. I am so happy for him because it's never easy to come here in the first year and win the title. He deserves it because he works hard every day."

Chelsea's David Luiz on his manager, Antonio Conte.[32]

With the title race over, attention turns to the remaining relegation place and to the battle for Champions League places. Despite a valiant effort under their new manager, Marco Silva, it's Hull City that fill the final relegation berth as they lose 4–0 away at Crystal Palace and join Sunderland and Middlesbrough in the drop to the Championship.

> **"Marco Silva has done a fantastic job since he came in. We were in a bad situation and he has done remarkably well to give us half a chance. But we just came up short."**
>
> Michael Dawson, Hull City captain[33]

It's also the last ever game at Tottenham's White Hart Lane before the stadium is demolished and replaced with a new 61,000-seater ground. In a fitting finale, Spurs beat Manchester United 2–1 and end the season with an unbeaten home record. Mauricio Pochettino's team finish in second place – the first time they've finished above neighbours Arsenal since 1995.

> **"I've never felt the connection so deeply between the fans and the players in a stadium."**
>
> Former Spurs' striker and one of the guests of honour at the game, Jurgen Klinsmann.[34]

The only outstanding matter to be resolved on the final day of the season is fourth place and the final Champions League spot, with Manchester City, Liverpool and Arsenal all in contention. But as City hammer Watford 5–0 and Jurgen Klopp's team stroll to a comfortable 3–0 win over Middlesbrough, it's Arsenal that miss out on a place in the competition for the first time since the 1995/96 season.

> *"It's very sad ... Overall I believe we played since January in a very difficult environment for different reasons. Some, obviously, you know about and that is very difficult for a group of players to cope with. Some others we will talk about another day. The psychological environment for the group of players was absolutely horrendous."*
>
> Arsène Wenger and how the ongoing debate about his future contributed to Arsenal's downfall.[35]

Though they miss out on the top four again, Manchester United book their place in the Champions League by winning the Europa League, beating Ajax 2-0 in the final in Stockholm.

At Stamford Bridge, meanwhile, there's a party in progress as Chelsea steamroller Sunderland 5–1 in their final game. The victory means Chelsea have secured 30 wins from their 38 games – a new Premier League record.

It's also a celebration of the career of their skipper, John Terry, whose 22-year association with the club finally comes to an end. In the 26th minute of the match, Terry (shirt number 26) is substituted and given a guard of honour by his Chelsea teammates before returning to the field at the end of the game to lift the Premier League trophy with Gary Cahill.

> **"[You are] The best supporters in the world without a doubt. You have given me everything. From the age of 14 when I signed, you picked me up when I was down, you sung my name when I had bad games and disappointed you. Thank you will never ever be enough. I am going to come back here one day, supporting this team. From the bottom of my heart, thank you. I love you all."**
>
> John Terry pours his heart out on the Stamford Bridge pitch.[36]

But not everybody is happy with the pre-planned stoppage in play.

> **"This isn't Hollywood, this is a Premier League fixture. I'm just a little bit bemused. This has obviously been set up and I'm a bit uncomfortable with it to be honest with you."**
>
> BBC pundit Garth Crooks[37]

The final word, however, goes to the Chelsea manager, Antonio Conte, who, in one spectacular season, has turned the team round and won his fourth league title in succession, after a hat trick of wins with Juventus.

> **"I dreamed this. I must be honest, if you ask me, my first day at Chelsea to arrive at the end of the season and to win the league ... it was very difficult for me to imagine this."**
>
> Antonio Conte, a league winner, yet again.[38]

Games Played: 38

Pos	Team	GD	Pts
1	Chelsea	+52	93
2	Tottenham Hotspur	+60	86
3	Manchester City	+41	78
4	Liverpool	+36	76
5	Arsenal	+33	75
6	Manchester United	+25	69
7	Everton	+18	61
8	Southampton	-7	46
9	Bournemouth	-12	46
10	West Bromwich Albion	-8	45
11	West Ham United	-17	45
12	Leicester City	-15	44
13	Stoke City	-15	44
14	Crystal Palace	-13	41
15	Swansea City	-25	41
16	Burnley	-16	40
17	Watford	-28	40
18	Hull City	-43	34
19	Middlesbrough	-26	28
20	Sunderland	-40	24

CHAMPIONS: Chelsea

RUNNERS-UP: Tottenham Hotspur

RELEGATED: Hull, Middlesbrough, Sunderland

PROMOTED: Newcastle United, Brighton and Hove Albion, Huddersfield Town

TOP GOALSCORER: Harry Kane, Tottenham Hotspur – 29

PLAYER OF THE SEASON: N'Golo Kanté, Chelsea

MANAGER OF THE SEASON: Antonio Conte, Chelsea

DID YOU KNOW? *Chelsea are the first club to win the English top-flight title on a Friday since Arsenal won it at Anfield in 1989.*

References

1992/93

1   BBC 5Live *In Short*/08/07/2015/Brian Deane/www.bbc.co.uk/programmes/p02z0lhx

2   Tony Gubba, *Match of the Day*

3   The Premier League/08/07/2015/Colin Hendry/www.premierleague.com/news/59526

4   *Mail Online*/12/08/2011/Martin Tyler/www.dailymail.co.uk/sport/
football/article-2024900/Martin-Tylers-20-favourite-Premier-League-
moments.html#ixzz4VGjObMn4%20Follow%20us:%20@MailOnline%20on%20
Twitter%20|%20DailyMail%20on%20Facebook

5   LFCTV *Thursday Night Show*/02/12/2016/Ronny Rosenthal

6   Eric Cantona, press statement

7   Howard Kendall

8   Sir Alex Ferguson 14/5/1993

10 *Shropshire Star*/02/09/2013/www.shropshirestar.com/sport/2013/02/09/shropshire-
stars-dalian-atkinson/

10 *Shropshire Star*/02/09/2013/www.shropshirestar.com/sport/2013/02/09/shropshire-
stars-dalian-atkinson/

11 Sir Alex Ferguson 14/5/1993

12 *The Sun*/08/05/2013/Shaun Custis/www.thesun.co.uk/archives/football/717185/my-
magic-moment-in-fergie-time

13 Sky Sports/25/07/2015/Jefferson Lake/www.skysports.com/football/
news/11662/9921006/referee-john-hilditch-on-the-birth-of-fergie-time-
andmanchester-united-glory-in-1993

14 *The Independent*/26/04/1993/Joe Lovejoy/www.independent.co.uk/sport/football-
a-driving-force-moulded-by-fierce-disappointment-as-forest-bid-farewell-tobrian-
clough-joe-1457775.html

15 *The Guardian*/01/05/1993/www.theguardian.com/sport/2007/jan/07/features.sport10

16 BBC Sport/02/05/2013/Chris Bevan/www.bbc.co.uk/sport/football/22317376

17   *The Independent*/08/05/1993/Owen Slot/www.independent.co.uk/sport/football-oldham-triumph-against-the-odds-royles-men-produce-the-performance-toensure-survival-as-2321704.html

18   *The Independent*/02/05/1993/Joe Lovejoy/www.independent.co.uk/news/manchester-united-are-league-champions-again-after-26-years-2320633.html

1993/94

1   Bass Brewery, company statement/20/02/1993

2   Manchester United/18/03/2012/Adam Marshall/www.manutd.com/en/News-And-Features/Features/2012/Mar/classic-manchester-united-archive-interview-withroy-keane.aspx?pageNo=3

3   *This is Wiltshire*/02/12/2015/Michael Reeves/www.thisiswiltshire.co.uk/news/headlines/14116150.IN_DEPTH_WITH___John_Gorman/?ref=mr&dp=35

4   *The Guardian*/08/05/2013/www.theguardian.com/football/2013/may/08/sir-alex-ferguson-best-quotes

5   *The Independent*/07/03/1994/Guy Hodgson/www.independent.co.uk/sport/football-ferguson-has-no-clues-about-chelsea-mystery-1427626.html

6   Martin Tyler, Sky Sports

7   *The Independent*/05/12/1993/Matthew Kelly and Dave Hadfield/www.independent.co.uk/sport/football-kendall-quits-goodison-1465430.html

8   The Anfield Wrap/11/03/2016/Simon Hughes/www.theanfieldwrap.com/2016/03/graeme-souness-where-it-all-went-wrong-for-me-at-liverpool/

9   *The Independent*/22/11/1993/Jon Culley/www.independent.co.uk/sport/football-cole-collects-hat-trick-to-humble-liverpool-strikers-display-their-talents-asnewcastles-1506052.html

10 *The Independent*/20/03/1994/Ian Ridley/www.independent.co.uk/sport/footballkeegan-salutes-coles-quality-1430313.html?amp

11 *Sky Sports*/09/11/2016/James Dale/www.skysports.com/football/news/11661/10652080/sir-alex-ferguson-says-breaking-up-1994-man-united-side-was-difficult

12 *The Independent*/01/01/1995/Ian Ridley/www.independent.co.uk/sport/supportiveness-of-the-fans-is-my-happiest-memory-mike-walker-the-escape-routeand-the-exit-door-1566250.html

13 *CFCnet.com*/23/08/2009/www.cfcnet.co.uk/2009/08/the-premiership-years-1993-1994/

14   *This is Wiltshire*/02/12/2015/Michael Reeves www.thisiswiltshire.co.uk/news/
     headlines/14116150.IN_DEPTH_WITH___John_Gorman/?ref=mr&lp=35

1994/95

1   Jurgen Klinsmann, press conference

2   *FourFourTwo*/29/07/2014/Steve Anglesey

3   *The Guardian*/27/08/2014/Sachin Nakrani/www.theguardian.com/football/blog/2014/
     aug/27/robbie-fowler-liverpool-arsenal-premier-league-quickest-hat-trick

4   *Birmingham Mail*/05/04/2011/www.birminghammail.co.uk/sport/football/football-
     news/ex-aston-villa-star-paul-151906

5   The National/05/01/2010/Andrew Cole/www.thenational.ae/sport/football/my-
     window-of-opportunity#page1

6   ESPN/10/01/2013/Jon Carter/en.espn.co.uk/football/sport/story/187567.html

7   Manchester United fans

8   *The Telegraph*/22/01/2015/www.telegraph.co.uk/sport/football/teams/manchester-
     united/11360502/Eric-Cantona-kick-Where-are-they-now.html This seems to be the
     source

9   Eric Cantona, press statement

10   Gordon Strachan, press conference

11   Arsenal FC, club statement

12   George Graham, press statement/22/02/1995

13   Tim Flowers, post-match interview/Sky Sports

14   Tony Gubba, BBC *Match of the Day*

15   *Mail Online*/02/04/2011/Sami Mokbel/www.dailymail.co.uk/sport/football/
     article-1372472/West-Ham-Man-United-1995-Ludek-Miklosko.html

16   *Mail Online*/02/04/2011/Sami Mokbel/www.dailymail.co.uk/sport/football/
     article-1372472/West-Ham-Man-United-1995-Ludek-Miklosko.html

17   *The Mirror*/15/05/2015/Kenny Dalglish/www.mirror.co.uk/sport/football/news/
     kenny-dalglish-blackburns-1995-title-5703195

18   Alan Shearer/16/05/2015

1995/96

1   Alan Sugar

2   Tony Gubba, BBC *Match of the Day*

3   James Alexander Gordon, BBC5 Live

4   Alan Hansen, BBC *Match of the Day*

5   Martin Tyler, Sky Sports

6   *Yorkshire Evening Post*/17/08/2015/Phil Hay/www.yorkshireeveningpost.co.uk/sport/
     football/leeds-united/leeds-united-exclusive-yeboah-on-that-wonder-goal-20-years-
     ago-1-7414136

7   Martin Tyler, Sky Sports

8   *Yorkshire Evening Post*/17/08/2015/Phil Hay/www.yorkshireeveningpost.co.uk/sport/
     football/leeds-united/leeds-united-exclusive-yeboah-on-that-wonder-goal-20-years-
     ago-1-7414136

9   Jon Champion, BBC 5Live

10   Middlesbrough FC club statement

11   *Esquire*/May 2016/Sam Parker/newcastleunitedentertainers.esquire.co.uk

12   *Esquire*/May 2016/Sam Parker/newcastleunitedentertainers.esquire.co.uk

13   *The Guardian*/25/06/2011/Stuart Jeffries/www.theguardian.com/theguardian/2011/
     jun/25/kevin-keegan-footballer-manager-liverpool

14   *The Independent*/Ian Potts/02/04/1996/www.independent.co.uk/sport/magpies-
     faltering-pursuit-of-silver-1303106.html

15   Martin Tyler, Sky Sports

16   Martin Tyler, Sky Sports

17   *Mail Online*/01/04/2016/Dominic King and Craig Hall/www.dailymail.co.uk/sport/
     football/article-3519573/Liverpool-4-3-Newcastle-United-20-years-talk-starsstaged-
     Premier-League-s-GREATEST-GAME-ALL.html

18   *Mail Online*/01/04/2016/Dominic King and Craig Hall/www.dailymail.co.uk/sport/
     football/article-3519573/Liverpool-4-3-Newcastle-United-20-years-talk-starsstaged-
     Premier-League-s-GREATEST-GAME-ALL.html

19   Martin Tyler, Sky Sports

20   Martin Tyler, Sky Sports

21   Martin Tyler, Sky Sports

22   Martin Tyler, Sky Sports

23   Martin Tyler, Sky Sports

24   Sky Sports/03/04/2009/Stan Collymore/www.skysports.com/football/
     news/11661/10249826/liverpool-4-3-newcastle-remembering-the-1996-premier-
     league-classic

25   Roy Evans, post-match interview/04/04/1996/Sky Sports

26   Sky Sports/30/07/2015/Jamie Redknapp/www.skysports.com/football/
news/18932/9905969/premier-league-moments-jamie-redknapp-picks-anfield-epic

27   *The Guardian*/25/06/2016/Stuart Jeffries/www.theguardian.com/theguardian/2011/
jun/25/kevin-keegan-footballer-manager-liverpool

28   Sir Alex Ferguson, post-match interview/15/04/1996/Sky Sports

29   *The Guardian*/15/04/2006/Lee Sharpe/www.theguardian.com/football/2006/apr/15/
sport.comment2

30   Kevin Keegan, post-match interview/Sky Sports

31   Nick Collins/Sky Sports

32   Sky Sports/29/04/2016/David Beckham

33   Tony Gubba, BBC *Match of the Day*

34   Niall Quinn, post-match interview/BBC Sport

35   Gary Neville/Sky Sports

36   *The Daily Telegraph*/20/01/2008/Colin Malam/www.telegraph.co.uk/sport/
football/2289437/Why-Keegans-class-of-96-blew-a-12-point-lead.html

37   Kevin Keegan/02/05/2014

38   *The Daily Telegraph*/12/09/2013/Mark Ogden/www.telegraph.co.uk/sport/
football/10287415/Alan-Hansen-claims-the-infamous-statement-about-Manchester-
Uniteds-kids-made-him-as-a-pundit.html

1996/97

1   Kevin Keegan, press statement/29/07/1996

2   *The Independent*/29/07/1996/Simon Turnbull and Alan Nixon/www.independent.
co.uk/sport/shearer-goes-home-for-pounds-15m-1331235.html

3   Sir Alex Ferguson, post-match interview/17/08/1996/Sky Sports

4   *The Sun*/21/04/2016/Andrew Richardson/www.thesun.co.uk/archives/
football/1138498/fabrizio-ravanelli-reveals-it-would-be-his-dream-to-manage-
clubof-his-heart-middlesbrough-in-premier-league/

5   Ian Wright

6   *The Guardian*/12/02/2000/Hunter Davies/www.theguardian.com/football/2000/
feb/12/newsstory.sport

7   *The Independent*/23/09/1996/Glenn Moore/www.independent.co.uk/sport/agraduate-
of-the-global-game-1364848.html

8   ESPN FC/04/10/2012/Jon Carter/www.espnfc.co.uk/story/1178984/rewind-to-1996-arsene-who

9   Sabotage Times/04/10/2010/Matt Weiner/sabotagetimes.com/football/arsene-wenger-most-of-my-idols-were-german

10   Arsène Wenger, press conference/23/09/1996

11   *The Telegraph*/21/03/2014/Henry Winter/www.telegraph.co.uk/sport/football/teams/arsenal/10715653/Chelsea-v-Arsenal-Arsene-Wenger-still-in-unceasingpursuit-of-perfection-after-1000-games-in-charge.html

12   Arsenal website/13/08/2015/Rob Kelly/www.arsenal.com/news/newsarchive/20150813/wenger-the-story-of-the-vieira-signing

13   Kevin Keegan, press conference/06/12/2013

14   *The Telegraph*/18/10/2013/Mark Ogden/www.telegraph.co.uk/sport/football/teams/manchester-united/10388255/Flashback-Southampton-6-Manchester-United-3-Egil-Ostenstad-scores-hat-trick-as-United-humbled-at-The-Dell.html

15   *The Sun*/20/12/2016/David Coverdale/www.thesun.co.uk/sport/2447711/ericcantonas-iconic-goal-shouldnt-even-exist-says-the-man-who-conceded-it-lionel-perez/

16   *The Guardian*/22/11/2008/*www.theguardian.com/football/blog/2008/nov/22/southampton-championship*

17   *Gazzetta dello Sport*/15/01/1997

18   *The Guardian*/19/12/2009/Tony Parkes/www.theguardian.com/sport/2009/dec/19/tony-parkes-blackburn-middlesbrough-flu

19   Kevin Keegan, press statement

20   *Chronicle Live*/06/01/2016/David Morton www.chroniclelive.co.uk/news/history/newcastle-united-shock-kevin-keegan-10687357

21   John Reagan/09/01/1997

22   Alan Parry, Sky Sports commentator

23   *The Guardian*/31/07/2014/Omar Saleem/www.theguardian.com/football/these-football-times/2014/jul/31/middlesbrough-transfers-changed-english-footballjuninho-emerson-ravanelli

24   *The Guardian*/25/03/2012/Julian Coman/www.theguardian.com/football/2012/mar/25/king-and-i-eric-cantona

25   *The Independent*/18/04/2009/Robert Chalmers/www.independent.co.uk/arts-entertainment/films/features/the-big-match-what-happened-when-good-socialist-ken-loach-met-eric-cantona-a-legend-of-one-of-the-1669047.html

1997/98

1   Joe Kinnear, press conference/07/09/1997

2   *The Guardian*/05/02/2006/Andrew Anthony/www.theguardian.com/sport/2006/
    feb/05/features.sport9

3   Terry Sheringham, post-match interview/10/08/1997/Sky Sports

4   *Leicester Mercury*/27/06/2009/Steve Walsh/www.leicestermercury.co.uk/steve-walsh-
    s-classicmatch-8211-bergkamp-brilliant-leicester-city-laugh/story-12093144-detail/
    story.Html

5   Arsenal.com/23/04/2014/www.arsenal.com/news/features/20140423/1997/98

6   Christian Gross, press conference

7   *The Independent*/20/11/1997/Glenn Moore/www.independent.co.uk/sport/sugar-
    didnt-want-me-to-go-francis-1295175.html

8   Jurgen Klinsmann, press conference/28/12/1997

9   Ruud Gullit, press conference/13/02/1998

10 Gianluca Vialli, press statement

11 Arsène Wenger, press conference/14/03/1998

12 Sir Alex Ferguson, press conference/14/03/1998

13 Martin Tyler, Sky Sports

14 Arsène Wenger, post-match interview/22/05/1998/Sky Sports

15 Lee Dixon, post-match interview/22/05/1998

1998/99

1   Alan Parry, Sky Sports

2   Ruud Gullit, post-match interview/30/08/1998/BBC Sport

3   *The Independent*/11/12/2011/Robert Chalmers/www.independent.co.uk/news/people/
    profiles/paolo-di-canio-my-life-speaks-for-me-6273526.html

4   *The Guardian*/05/09/2009/John Scales/www.theguardian.com/sport/2009/sep/05/
    christian-gross-tottenham-hotspur-fired

5   *The Independent*/27/10/2000/Glenn Moore/www.independent.co.uk/sport/football/
    premier-league/graham-fights-to-escape-that-arsenal-thing-637562.html

6   Peter Ridsdale, press conference/18/10/1998

7   Roy Evans, press conference/12/11/1998

8   Brian Kidd, press conference/13/05/1999

9   Brian Kidd, press conference/13/05/1999

10   Arsène Wenger, press conference/11/05/1999

11   Sir Alex Ferguson, post-match interview/Sky Sports

1999/00

1   Sir Alex Ferguson, press statement/30/06/1999

2   Sir Alex Ferguson, press conference/30/06/1999

3   Dennis Wise

4   Arsène Wenger, press conference/03/08/1999

5   Arsenal.com/16/12/2014/www.arsenal.com/news/features/20141211/thierryhenry#vQ LhiDHFoLCA2Zbi.99

6   *Manchester Evening News*/02/11/2016/Ciaran Kelly/www.manchestereveningnews. co.uk/sport/football/football-news/manchester-united-news-massimo-taibi-12108631

7   *The Guardian*/10/10/1999/Ian Ridley/www.theguardian.com/football/1999/oct/10/ newsstory.sport8

8   Alan Shearer, post-match interview/19/09/1999/BBC Sport

9   *The Mirror*/02/02/2017/Adrian Kajumba/www.mirror.co.uk/sport/football/news/ arsenal-head-chelsea-nwankwo-kanu-9747755

10   Peter Ridsdale, press statement

11   *The Express*/26/12/2014/Niall Hickman/www.express.co.uk/sport/football/548650/ Chelsea-s-non-British-starting-XI-Gianluca-Vialli-against-Southampton

12   *The Guardian*/16/02/2000/Donald McRae/www.theguardian.com/football/2000/ feb/16/newsstory.sport3

13   Martin Tyler, Sky Sports

14   *The Independent*/11/12/2016/www.independent.co.uk/news/people/profiles/paolo-di-canio-my-life-speaks-for-me-6273526.html

15   Sir Alex Ferguson, post-match interview/22/04/2000

16   David Leary, press conference/14/05/2000

17   Martin Tyler, Sky Sports

18   David Wetherall, post-match interview/14/05/2000/BBC Sport

2000/01

1   *Leicester Mercury*/10/07/2015/www.leicestermercury.co.uk/heart-soul-leicestercity-martin-o-neill/story-26878382-detail/story.html

2   Sky Sports/25/11/2015/www.skysports.com/football/news/11712/10078181/thelast-time-leicester-were-top "

3   Arsène Wenger, press conference/02/10/2000

4   Sir Alex Ferguson, post-match interview/02/10/2000/Sky Sports

5   Martin Tyler, Sky Sports

6   Mark Viduka, post-match interview/Sky Sports

7   ITV/04/10/2014/www.itv.com/news/calendar/topic/leeds-united/?page=38

8   Roy Keane/24/08/2006

9   Everton website/19/04/2013/www.evertonfc.com/news/2013/04/19/gerrardrecalls-di-canio-catch

10 Walter Smith, post-match interview/17/12/2000

11 Arsène Wenger, post-match interview/21/02/2001

12 www.manutd.com/21/02/2001//en/EditorialNews/NewsStory.aspx?session=&mx=&page=0&NewsId=15052085

13 *The Guardian*/13/08/2002/www.theguardian.com/football/2002/aug/13/sport

14 *The Telegraph*/28/10/2008/Rod Gilmour/www.telegraph.co.uk/sport/football/teams/manchester-united/3272875/Alex-Ferguson-Paolo-Di-Canio-wouldhave-been-a-Manchester-United-great-Football.html

15 Matthew Le Tissier, post-match interview/21/05/2001/Match of the Day

16 Arsène Wenger, post-match interview/19/05/2001/Sky Sports

17 Henry Winter/20/04/2001/www.telegraph.co.uk/sport/football/teams/manchester-city/3003700/On-The-Spot-Joe-Royle.html

18 Gordon Strachan, post-match interview/05/07/2001

19 LiverpoolFC.com/06/12/2010

20 Sir Alex Ferguson, club statement/18/05/2001

21 Planet Football/19/01/2017/Steven Chicken/www.planetfootball.com/in-depth/story-george-burley-remarkable-ipswich-team-2000/

2001/02

1   *Evening Standard*/05/09/2015/James Benge/www.standard.co.uk/sport/football/sol-campbell-tottenham-fans-still-havent-moved-on-over-my-arsenalswitch-a2927646.html

2   BBC Sport/24/05/2001/www.news.bbc.co.uk/sport1/hi/football/teams/m/man_city/1349333.stm

3   BBC Sport/24/05/2001/www.news.bbc.co.uk/sport1/hi/football/teams/m/man_
    city/1349333.stm

4   *The Telegraph*/26/08/2001/Matt Lawton and Henry Winter/www.telegraph.co.uk/
    sport/football/teams/manchester-united/3011533/Ferguson-writes-off-Stamfor-
    16.4m.html

5   Sir Alex Ferguson, press conference/26/05/2016

6   Sir Alex Ferguson, post-match interview/29/11/2001/Sky Sports

7   *The Telegraph*/29/11/2013/John Percy/www.telegraph.co.uk/sport/football/teams/
    manchester-united/10484491/The-day-Manchester-United-produced-theirgreatest-
    comeback-and-a-warning-for-Tottenham.html

8   Glenn Hoddle, post-match interview/01/10/2001/Sky Sports

9   Gordon Strachan, press conference/01/10/2001

10 Walter Smith, post-match interview/22/11/2001

11 *The Metro*/14/05/2016

12 Bobby Robson, post-match press conference/24/12/2001

13 Bobby Robson, post-match press conference/22/04/2002

14 David O'Leary, press statement/27/06/2002

15 Peter Ridsdale, press statement/10/02/2003

16 Sir Alex Ferguson, press statement/07/05/2002

17 Dave Bassett, post-match press conference/06/04/2002

18 David Sheepshanks, post-match press conference/13/05/2002

19 Arsenal FC fans

20 Sir Alex Ferguson, Manchester United programme notes/09/05/2002

21 Arsène Wenger, press conference/08/05/2002

22 *The Guardian*/12/05/2002/Kevin Mitchell/www.theguardian.com/football/2002/
    may/12/sport.comment4

2002/03

1   Peter Ridsdale, press conference/17/07/2002

2   Sir Alex Ferguson, press conference/22/07/2002

3   *The Guardian*/30/09/2002/Daniel Taylor/www.theguardian.com/football/2002/sep/30/
    match.leedsunited

4   Terry Venables, post-match press conference/29/09/2002

5   Arsène Wenger, post-match press conference/30/09/2002

6   Clive Tyldesley, ITV Sport commentary

7   *The Telegraph*/30/09/2002/Henry Winter/www.telegraph.co.uk/sport/football/teams/leeds-united/3035346/Henry-perfects-one-track-mind.html

8   *Liverpool Echo*/02/01/2003/www.liverpoolecho.co.uk/sport/football/footballnews/newcastle-1-liverpool-0-echo-3555628

9   Sunderland FC club statement

10 Manchester City fans

11 Kevin Keegan, post-match press conference/11/11/2002

12 Sir Alex Ferguson, post-match press conference/11/11/2002

13 David Beckham, post-match press conference/04/11/2011

14 Mick McCarthy, press announcement/13/03/2003

15 Sir Alex Ferguson, press conference/07/05/2012

16 Sir Alex Ferguson, press conference/05/05/2003

17 Arsène Wenger, post-match press conference/05/05/2003

18 The Premier League/18/07/2015/Don Hutchison/www.premierleague.com/news/59655

2003/04

1   *Gazzetta dello Sport*/31/05/2007

2   *The Telegraph*/23/07/2003/Paul Hayward/www.telegraph.co.uk/sport/2408166/Chelsea-spending-spree-revives-the-silly-season.html

3   Cristiano Ronaldo, press presentation/13/08/2003

4   *The Guardian*/13/08/2003/Daniel Taylor/www.theguardian.com/football/2003/aug/13/newsstory.sport10

5   Sir Alex Ferguson, post-match press conference/17/08/2003

6   Sam Allardyce, post-match press conference/18/08/2003/Daniel Taylor

7   *The Independent*/15/02/2008/Brian Viner/www.independent.co.uk/sport/football/fa-league-cups/martin-keown-i-rang-my-wife-after-the-game-shes-usuallyvery-supportive-but-she-said-i-think-youve-782328.html

8   Ruud van Nistelrooy, Oxford Union conference/25/11/2015

9   Sir Alex Ferguson, press conference/17/10/2004

10 Daniel Levy, club statement/22/09/2003

11   Peter Reid, post-match interview/10/11/2003/BBC Sport

12   Eddie Gray, press conference/10/11/2003

13   *The Guardian*/25/04/2004/Amy Lawrence/www.theguardian.com/football/2004/apr/25/arsenal

14   Goal/17/02/2017/www.goal.com/en-gb/news/683/main/2017/02/17/32775692/please-retire-arsene-before-you-destroy-everything

15   *Metro*/08/11/2016/Chris Davie/metro.co.uk/2016/11/08/gary-neville-i-wantedmanchester-united-to-sign-louis-saha-after-he-destroyed-me-6243536/

16   *The Telegraph*/19/12/2014/Jeremy Wilson/www.telegraph.co.uk/sport/11305343/Liverpool-vs-Arsenal-The-day-Thierry-Henry-got-Arsenals-Invincibles-back-on-track.html

17   Eddie Gray, post-match interview/03/05/2004/BBC Sport

18   Thierry Henry, post-match interview/25/04/2004/BBC Sport

19   Arsène Wenger, post-match interview/25/04/2004/Sky Sports

20   Arsène Wenger, post-match interview/15/05/2004

2004/05

1   Michael Owen, press statement/14/08/2004

2   Jose Mourinho, press conference/03/06/2013

3   Wayne Rooney, press conference/31/08/2004

4   Sir Alex Ferguson, press conference/31/08/2004

5   Sir Bobby Robson, press conference/30/08/2004

6   Jose Mourinho, post-match press conference/08/09/2004

7   *London Evening Standard*/26/10/2004/Valentine Low/www.standard.co.uk/sport/who-hit-sir-alex-with-pizza-6955390.html

8   *The Sun*/13/12/2016/Gavin Newsham/www.thesun.co.uk/sport/football/2385681/premier-league-christmas-advent-calendar-december-13-pizzagaterocks-the-premier-league-after-manchester-united-beat-arsenal

9   ITV/09/12/2013

10   Chelsea FC, club statement/29/10/2004

11   Ashely Cole, post-match interview/15/11/2004/Sky Sports

12   Jose Mourinho, press conference/15/11/2004

13   Jose Mourinho, press conference/31/10/2005

14 *Mail Online*/25/05/2016/Sam Cunningham/www.dailymail.co.uk/sport/football/
article-3608853/Jose-Mourinho-Sir-Alex-Ferguson-enjoyed-closefriendship-similar-
views-football-wine-bond-grow-closer-Man-United.html

15 Pedro Mendes, post-match interview/05/01/2005/Sky Sports

16 *Mail Online*/24/04/2010/Chris Wheeler/www.dailymail.co.uk/sport/football/
article-1268332/Roy-Carroll-Pedro-Mendes-linesman--forget-Spurs-phantom-goal.
Html

17 Jose Mourinho, press conference/31/10/2005

18 Arsène Wenger, press conference/15/02/2005

19 Delia Smith, public announcement

20 Manchester City club statement

21 Eurosport/24/10/2014/www.eurosport.co.uk/football/bowyer-regrets-dyer-clash_
sto4450229/story.shtml

22 *Chronicle Live*/20/10/2014/Lee Ryder//football-news/kieron-dyer-lifts-lid-
fight-7968397

23 David Moyes, post-match press conference/12/05/2005

24 Bryan Robson, post-match interview/15/05/2005/BBC Sport

25 Jose Mourinho, post-match press conference/31/10/2005

2005/06

1 BBC Sport/31/08/2005/www.news.bbc.co.uk/sport1/hi/football/teams/n/newcastle_
united/4199526.stm

2 Jose Mourinho, post-match press conference/15/11/2016

3 Arsène Wenger, press conference/22/09/2016

4 Jose Mourinho, post-match press conference/15/11/2016

5 Thierry Henry, post-match press conference/22/10/2005

6 *The Independent*/18/02/2016/Samuel Stevens/www.independent.co.uk/sport/football/
premier-league/robert-pires-sets-record-straight-with-danny-mills-ondisrespectful-
penalty-a6881011.html

7 *Mail Online*/17/12/2010/Chris Wheeler/www.dailymail.co.uk/sport/football/
article-1339613/Darren-Fletcher-Scoring-Chelsea-set-way-Manchester-United.
html

8 Jose Mourinho, press conference/17/12/2015

9   Harry Redknapp, press conference/18/01/2006

10   Gary Neville/24/01/2006/*The Times*

11   Jamie Carragher, press conference/24/01/2006

12   Thierry Henry, post-match interview/16/01/2006

13   Steve McCLaren, post-match interview/14/01/2006/BBC Sport

14   Southampton club statement/20/01/2006

15   Harry Redknapp

16   Arsène Wenger, press conference/13/10/2015/Adam Shergold/

17   *The Independent*/13/10/2015/Tom Sheen/www.independent.co.uk/sport/football/
     premier-league/ashley-cole-was-right-to-ditch-arsenal-for-chelsea-asgunners-
     didnt-win-anything-says-agent-a6692001.html

18   BBC Sport/22/04/2006/www.news.bbc.co.uk/sport1/hi/football/teams/n/newcastle_
     united/4929358.stm

19   José Mourinho, post match-interview/01/05/2006/Sky Sports

20   *The Guardian*/20/04/2006/Jeremy Wilson/www.theguardian.com/football/2006/
     apr/29/sport.comment2

21   *Yahoo.com*/01/03/2016/Jermaine Jenas

22   Arsenal website/05/05/2006/www.arsenal.com/news/news-archive/bergkandgets-one-
     last-opportunity-at-highbury

23   Thierry Henry, post-match interview/Sky Sports

2006/07

1   Denis Bergkamp, press conference/22/07/2006

2   West Ham United, club statement

3   Jose Mourihno, press conference/31/05/2006/Sky Sports

4   Sir Alex Ferguson, post-match interview/21/08/2006/Sky Sports

5   Harry Redknapp, post-match interview/16/09/2006/Sky Sports

6   BBC Sport/25/08/2006/www.news.bbc.co.uk/sport1/hi/football/teams/p/
     portsmouth/5284422.stm

7   Stuart Pearce, post-match press conference/01/01/2007

8   Rafa Benitez, post-match press conference/20/09/2006

9   *The Telegraph*/02/10/2006/Martin Smith/www.telegraph.co.uk/sport/football/2347045/
     Barton-blue-moon-under-investigation-by-police.html

10   Ian Holloway, press conference/06/10/2006

11   Sky Sports/29/10/2016/Patrick Davison/www.skysports.com/football/
news/11095/10635543/petr-cech-on-brush-with-death-at-reading-it-was-a-
veryclose-call

12   talkSPORT/22/12/2011/Michael Wade/talksport.com/radio/hawksbee-andjacobs/
blog/2011-12-22/moritz-volz-reflects-scoring-15000th-premier-league-
goal9781472946935

13   Paul Robinson, post-match interview/19/03/2007/BBC Sport

14   Ben Foster, post-match interview/19/03/2007/BBC Sport

15   Peter Crouch, post-match interview/02/04/2007/Sky Sports

16   Arsène Wenger, post-match interview/02/04/2007/Sky Sports

17   Sir Alex Ferguson, press conference/14/05/2007

18   *The Guardian*/17/03/2009/Owen Gibson/www.theguardian.com/football/2009/mar/17/
carlos-tevez-west-ham-sheffield-united-neil-warnock

19   Sir Alex Ferguson, press conference/06/05/2007

2007/08

1   Goal/01/02/2005/Chris Davie/www.goal.com/en/news/9/englishfootball/
2015/02/01/8517962/henry-i-cried-when-i-left-arsenal-for-barcelona

2   José Mourinho, press conference/20/09/2007

3   Sir Alex Ferguson, post-match press conference/16/08/2007

4   Billy Davies, post-match press conference/01/09/2007

5   Steve Coppell, post-match press conference/23/07/2015

6   Chelsea FC club statement

7   Jose Mourinho, press conference/25/09/07

8   Sky Sports/12/05/2008/www.skysports.com/football/news/11668/2741782/wilkins-
no-sense-in-jose-exit

9   Jose Mourinho, press conference/15/03/2010

10   Avram Grant, press conference/25/09/2007

11   BBC 5Live/20/09/2007/www.news.bbc.co.uk/sport1/hi/football/teams/c/
chelsea/7004083.stm

12   Ian Holloway, post-match interview/28/09/2007

13   Avram Grant, post-match interview/25/09/2007/BBC Sport

14 BBC 5Live/12/05/2008/Chris Charles/www.news.bbc.co.uk/sport1/hi/funny_old_
    game/7389986.stm

15 *The Telegraph*/14/11/2007/John Ley/www.telegraph.co.uk/sport/football/2325705/
    Arsenal-amaze-Dave-Kitson.html

16 Billy Davies, post-match press conference/25/11/2007

17 Paul Jewell, post-match press conference/12/05/2008

18 BBC 5Live/25/12/2008

19 Sam Allardyce, press conference/22/07/2016

20 Steve Bruce, press conference/26/12/2008

21 News Talk/12/05/2008

22 BBC Sport/04/04/2008/news.bbc.co.uk/sport1/hi/football/7329117.stm

23 Arsène Wenger, post-match press conference/24/2/2008

24 Michel Platini, UEFA press conference/20/05/2009

25 Roy Hodgson, post-match interview/12/05/2008/BBC Sport

26 Steve Coppell, post-match interview/12/05/2008/BBC Sport

27 *Mail Online*/17/11/2012/Gary Neville/www.dailymail.co.uk/sport/football/
    article-2234511/Gary-Neville-Brave-ruthless-relentless-Ronaldo-redefined-football.
    Html

28 *Mail Online*/28/03/2015/Oliver Todd/www.dailymail.co.uk/sport/football/
    article-3015920/Chelsea-captain-John-Terry-haunted-penalty-miss-2008-
    Champions-League-final-against-Manchester-United.html

2008/09

1 Chelsea FC club statement

2 Luiz Felipe Scolari, press conference/12/06/2008

3 Khaldoon Al Mubarak, press statement/23/09/2008

4 Mark Hughes, press statement/01/09/2008

5 Kevin Keegan, press statement/04/09/2008

6 Joe Kinnear, press conference/26/09/2008

7 Joe Kinnear, press conference/03/10/2008

8 *The Telegraph*/25/09/2008/Richard Bright/www.telegraph.co.uk/sport/football/
   competitions/premier-league/3081374/Hulls-Phil-Brown-has-no-fear-of-Arsenal-
   Football.html

9   BBC 5Live/26/10/2008/www.news.bbc.co.uk/sport1/hi/football/7691457.stm

10   Jamie Carragher, post-match interview/26/10/2008/Sky Sports

11   Martin Tyler, Sky Sports commentary

12   David Bentley, post-match interview/BBC Sport

13   Harry Redknapp, press conference/05/11/2008

14   Sir Alex Ferguson, post-match press conference/06/11/2016

15   Phil Brown, post-match press conference/31/12/2008

16   *FourFourTwo*/16/05/2014/Andrew Murray/www.fourfourtwo.com/features/
     geovanni-i-was-proud-when-hull-beat-arsenal-its-dream-see-them-
     cupfinal#CaFmjPpL350rpxuk.99

17   Manchester City Fan tattoo

18   Rafa Benítez, press conference/09/01/2009

19   Sir Alex Ferguson, post-match press conference/12/01/2009

20   John Terry, press conference/11/02/2009

21   Alan Shearer, press conference/02/04/2009

22   Martin Tyler, Sky Sports

23   Arsène Wenger, post-match press conference/22/04/2009

24   Alan Shearer, press conference/24/05/2009

2009/10

1   Cristiano Ronaldo, press conference/06/07/2009

2   Sir Alex Ferguson, press conference/20/07/2009

3   Erected sign, Deansgate, Manchester city centre

4   Sir Alex Ferguson, post-match press conference/08/05/2013

5   Carlo Ancelotti, press conference/01/06/2009

6   Managing Madrid website/28/06/2013/J A Marsano/www.managingmadrid.c
     om/2013/6/28/4473048/in-his-own-words-carlo-ancelotti

7   Sky Sports/18/05/2010

8   *Manchester Evening News*/29/10/2014/James Robson/www.manchestereveningnews.
     co.uk/sport/football/football-news/michael-owenremembers-derby-goal-8014125

9   Mark Hughes, post-match interview/21/09/2009

10   Darren Bent, post-match interview/18/10/2009/BBC Sport

11 *The Telegraph*/09/01/2015/Jim White/www.telegraph.co.uk/sport/football/
teams/liverpool/11336948/Liverpool-beware-the-beach-balls-against-Sunderland.
html

12 Phil Brown, post-match press conference/29/11/2009

13 Jermaine Defoe, post-match interview/23/11/2009

14 Roberto Martinez, post-match press conference/12/12/2009

15 Mark Hughes, press conference/09/09/2013

16 Roberto Mancini, press conference/21/12/2009

17 Burnley supporters' chant

18 Alan Parry, Sky Sports

19 Arsène Wenger, post-match interview/27/02/2010/Sky Sports

20 *The Guardian*/03/04/2010/Paul Wilson/www.theguardian.com/football/2010/apr/03/
manchester-united-chelsea-premier-league

21 Chelsea FC fan banner

22 Carlo Ancelotti, press conference/05/01/2010

2010/11

1 Goal.com/23/08/2010/Anthony Sciarrino/www.goal.com/en/news/9/english-
football/2010/08/23/2083185/florent-malouda-insists-chelsea-have-stepped-their-
game-up

2 Ian Holloway, post-match interview/28/05/2013

3 Sam Allardyce, post-match press conference/29/11/2010

4 *The Independent*/28/05/2011/Phil Shaw/www.independent.co.uk/sport/football/
premier-league/talking-a-good-game-footballing-quotes-of-the-season-2290496.html

5 Manchester city centre graffiti

6 Sir Alex Ferguson, press conference/25/10/2010

7 Wayne Rooney, press statement/22/10/2010

8 LFC TV/28/05/2011

9 Gary Neville, press statement/02/02/2011

10 BBC 5Live/31/01/2011/news.bbc.co.uk/sport1/hi/football/teams/l/liverpool/9382215.
stm

11 Alan Pardew, post-match press conference/05/02/2011

12 Arsène Wenger, post-match press conference/05/02/2011

13   Roberto Mancini, post-match conference/13/02/2011

14   Sir Alex Ferguson, post-match press conference/13/02/2011

15   Manchester United fan chant

16   BBC Sport/03/04/2011/www.bbc.co.uk/news/mobile/uk-england-london-12950708

17   Sir Alex Ferguson, addressing Old Trafford/22/05/2011

18   Sir Alex Ferguson/09/09/2002

2011/12

1   Brendan Rodgers, post-match press conference/25/08/2012

2   Alan Pardew, post-match interview/05/11/2011/Sky Sports

3   Arsène Wenger, post-match press conference/29/08/2011

4   *The Telegraph*/28/08/2011/Henry Winter/www.telegraph.co.uk/sport/football/
     competitions/premier-league/8722411/Manchester-United-8-Arsenal-2-matchreport.
     Html

5   Gazzetta TV/16/07/2015

6   Mario Balotelli 's T-shirt design

7   Noel Gallagher/31/12/2011

8   Luis Suarez, press conference in Montevideo/08/11/2011

9   A chant from Liverpool 's Kop

10   Sir Alex Ferguson, post-match press conference/11/02/2012

11   Kenny Dalglish, post-match press conference/11/02/2012

12   Gary Cahill 's T-shirt design

13   *The Sun*/21/04/2012/Nick Parker and Sharon Hendry/www.thesun.co.uk/archives/
     news/552560/fabrice-muamba-i-asked-god-to-protect-me-he-didntlet-me-down/

14   Roberto Mancini, post-match press conference/08/04/2012

15   Roberto Mancini, post-match press conference/08/04/2012

16   Martin Tyler, Sky Sports

17   Sergio Augero, post-match interview/14/05/2012/Sky Sports

18   Roberto Mancini, post-match press conference/13/05/2012

19   Sir Alex Ferguson, post-match interview/13/05/2012

20   *The Mirror*/13/05/2012/David McDonnell/www.mirror.co.uk/news/miraclescan-
     happen-on-the-other-side-of-manchester-831830

2012/13

1   *The Guardian*/17/08/2012/Stuart James/www.theguardian.com/football/2012/aug/17/michael-laudrup-swansea-philosophy

2   Roberto di Matteo, post-match press conference/28/10/2012

3   Sky Sports/28/10/2012

4   Sam Allardyce, press conference/03/11/2012

5   Chelsea FC club statement

6   Chelsea FC fan banners

7   Andre Villas-Boas, post-match press conference/28/11/2012

8   Paul Lambert, post-match press conference/23/12/2012

9   Theo Walcott, post-match press conference/04/01/2013

10 Paolo Di Canio, press conference/15/10/2015

11 BBC Wiltshire/08/03/2013

12 Topman promotional video/05/03/2013

13 BBC 5Live/19/05/2013

14 Prime Minister David Cameron/26/04/2013

15 Brendan Rodgers, post-match press conference/27/04/2013

16 Alan Pardew, post-match press conference/27/04/2013

17 Peter Drury, BBC Radio 5 Live

18 Robin Van Persie, post-match press conference/23/04/2013

19 Roberto Martinez, post-match press conference/15/05/2013

20 Steve Clarke, post-match press conference/19/05/2013

21 *The Mirror*/03/01/2014/Steve Anglesey/www.mirror.co.uk/sport/football/news/football-gaffes-2013-part-one-2975538

22 Rafa Benitez, post-match press conference/16/05/2013

2013/14

1   David Moyes, press conference/06/07/2013

2   Manchester United fan banner

3   Chelsea FC TV/03/06/2013

4   *The Independent*/04/06/2013/James Lawton/www.independent.co.uk/sport/football/news-and-comment/james-lawton-jose-mourinho-and-chelsea-a-love-storythat-was-destined-to-have-a-rerun-8643017.html

5   West Ham United, club statement/19/06/2013/Simon Rice/www.whufc.com

6   Arsène Wenger, pre-match press conference/08/11/2013

7   Sky Sports/16/10/2014/Peter Fraser/www.skysports.com/football/
    news/31671/9519215/the-world-according-to-paolo

8   TalkSport/12/08/2015

9   Asmir Begovic, post-match interview/02/11/2013/BBC Sport

10 Artur Boruc, post-match interview/02/11/2013/BBC Sport

11 Arsène Wenger, pre-match press conference/15/12/2013

12 Brendan Rodgers, pre-match press conference 04/12/2013

13 José Mourinho, post-match press conference/30/01/2014

14 Sam Allardyce, post-match press conference 29/01/2014

15 José Mourinho, post-match press conference/03/02/2014

16 Arsène Wenger, press conference/14/02/2014

17 José Mourinho, pre-match press conference/14/02/2014

18 Newcastle United club statement/11/03/2014

19 Professional Game Match Officials Limited statement/22/03/2014

20 David Moyes, post-match press conference/25/03/2014

21 Old Trafford plane fan banner

22 BBC 5Live/29/03/2014

23 *Manchester Evening News* newspaper Headline/22/04/2014/Peter Spencer/www.
    manchestereveningnews.co.uk/sport/david-moyes-manchester-united-sir-7015226

24 José Mourinho, post-match press conference/20/04/2014

25 *The Guardian*/13/04/2014/Daniel Taylor/www.theguardian.com/football/
    2014/apr/13/liverpool-manchester-city-premier-league-match-report

26 Martin Tyler, Sky Sports

27 Brendan Rodgers, post-match press conference/28/04/2014

28 Liverpool fans at Selhurst Park

29 Brendan Rodgers, post-match press conference/06/05/2014

30 *The Guardian*/06/05/2014/Daniel Taylor/www.theguardian.com/football/2014/
    may/05/crystal-palace-liverpool-premier-league-match-report

31 Manuel Pellegrini, post-match press conference/11/05/2014

32 Manchester City fan chant

33 BT Sport/24/06/2015

2014/15

1 Brendan Rodgers, press conference/25/05/2015

2 Louis van Gaal, pre-match press conference/22/11/2014

3 Louis van Gaal, post-match press conference/22/09/2014

4 Nigel Pearson, post-match press conference/22/09/2014

5 José Mourinho, press conference/25/07/2014

6 Frank Lampard, post-match interview/21/09/2014/Sky Sports

7 José Mourinho, post-match conference/21/09/2014

8 *Telefoot*/12/10/2014

9 José Mourinho, press conference/21/10/2015

10 Mauricio Pochettino, post-match press Conference/26/10/2014

11 Nigel Pearson, post-match press conference/30/04/2015

12 Nigel Pearson, post-match press conference/30/04/2015

13 BBC Sport/01/01/2015/www.bbc.com/sport/football/30652357.app

14 Nigel Pearson, post-match press conference/23/05/2015

15 John Carver, post-match press conference/23/05/2015

16 BBC Radio Solent/16/05/2015

17 *Metro*/22/05 2015/Colin Murray/metro.co.uk/2015/05/22/ronald-koemanshould-be-named-premier-league-manager-of-the-year-for-the-job-he-has-done-atsouthampton-this-season-5210603/

18 Brendan Rodgers, post-match press conference/24/05/2015

19 BT Sport/24/11/2016/Gary Lineker

20 Frank Lampard, post-match interview/24/05/2015/Sky Sports

21 Dick Advocaat, post-match press conference/10/05/2015

22 Nigel Pearson, post-match Press conference/24/05/2015

23 Sky Sports/03/05/2015

24 José Mourinho, post-match press conference/03/05/2015

2015/16

1 Gary Lineker, Twitter

2 *The Guardian*/14/07/2015/Marcus Christenson/www.theguardian.com/football/blog/2015/jul/14/claudio-ranieri-leicester-city-nigel-pearson

3   Sky Sports/31/05/2016/Oliver Yew/www.skysports.com/football/
    news/11661/10282956/quotes-of-the-season

4   Arsène Wenger, post-match press conference/19/09/2015

5   José Mourinho, post-match press conference/19/09/2015

6   Sky Sports/04/10/2015

7   Jurgen Klopp, press conference/31/05/2016

8   Claudio Ranieri, post-match press conference/31/05/2016

9   Christian Fuchs, Twitter/31/05/2016

10 José Mourinho, post-match press conference/14/12/2015

11 Chelsea FC club statement

12 BBC 5Live/17/12/2015

13 Claudio Ranieri, press conference/04/03/2016

14 Gary Lineker, Twitter

15 BBC Sport/24/01/2016/Garth Crooks/www.bbc.co.uk/sport/football/35396058?ns_
    mchannel=social&ns_campaign=bbc_match_of_the_day&ns_source=facebook&ns_
    linkname=sport

16 Marcus Rashford, post-match interview/28/02/2016/BBC Sport

17 Eddie Howe, post-match press conference/05/12/2015

18 Newcastle United club statement/11/03/2016/www.nufc.co.uk/news/archive/rafa-
    benitez-confirmed-as-newcastle-manager

19 Louis va Gaal, post-match press conference/23/12/2015

20 Louis va Gaal, post-match press conference/02/05/2016

21 Claudio Ranieri, post-match press conference/17/05/2016

22 Sky Sports/11/05/2016/Peter Smith/www.skysports.com/football/
    news/11685/10277251/west-hams-fond-farewell-to-the-boleyn-ground

23 Sky Sports/11/05/2016/Peter Smith/www.skysports.com/football/
    news/11685/10277251/west-hams-fond-farewell-to-the-boleyn-ground

24 Slaven Bilic, post-match press conference/11/05/2016

25 Sky Sports/07/05/2016

26 Sky Sports/31/05/2016/Oliver Yew/www.skysports.com/football/
    news/11661/10282956/quotes-of-the-season

27 *The Mirror*/07/05/2016/Tom Hopkinson/www.mirror.co.uk/sport/football/news/
    jamie-vardy-says-must-been-7921433

2016/17

1   Antonio Conte, press conference/14/07/2016

2   José Mourinho press statement

3   Pep Guardiola, press conference/08/07/2016

4   Manchester City club statement/25/08/2016

5   Manchester United club statement/09/08/2016

6   Slaven Bilic, pre-match press conference/03/08/2016

7   David Moyes, post-match interview/21/08/2016/Sky Sports

8   Gary Lineker, Twitter

9   Antonio Conte, pre-match press conference/03/02/2017

10   Jurgen Klopp, post-match press conference/03/02/2017

11   Arsène Wenger, pre-match press conference/30/09/2016

13   TalkSport/28/12/2016

14   Sam Allardyce, press conference/23/12/2016

15   Mauricio Pochettino, press conference/04/01/2017

16   Arsenal.com/10/01/2017

17   BBC Sport/14/01/2017/Tim Oscroft/www.bbc.co.uk/sport/football/38539427

18   Slaven Bilic, post-match press conference/14/01/2017

19   MUTV/21/01/2017

20   Leicester City club statement/23/02/2017

21   Claudio Ranieri press statement/24/02/2017

22   Gary Lineker, Twitter

23   Aitor Karanka press statement/16/03/2017

24   MUTV/04/03/2017

25   Tyrone Mings, Twitter

26   Antonio Conte, press conference/10/02/2017

27   José Mourinho, post-match interview/02/05/2017/Sky Sports

28   Sky Sports/02/05/2017

29   Paul Clement, post-match press conference/30/04/2017

30   Sky Sports/01/05/2017

31   Antonio Conte, post-match press conference/12/05/2017

32   BBC Sport/12/05/2017

33   Michael Dawson, post-match interview/14/05/2017

34   tottenhamhotspur.com/14/05/2017

35   Arsène Wenger, post-match press conference/21/05/2017

36   John Terry personal statement/21/05/2017

37   BBC Sport/21/05/2017

38   Sky Sports/21/05/2017

Gavin Newsham is a sportswriter and journalist who has written for *The Guardian, The Sunday Times, The Observer* and *The Sun*. He was awarded the National Sporting Club Best New Writer for his first book, *Letting the Big Dog Eat*. He has published eleven books on sport including *Once In A Lifetime: The Incredible Story of the New York Cosmos, Hype & Glory: The Decline and Fall of the England Football Team* and *The Official Treasures of Muhammad Ali*. He lives in Brighton.

The **National Football Museum** is the biggest and best football museum in the world and looks after over 200,000 objects for football fans everywhere. Since opening in Manchester in 2012 the museum has welcomed over 2.5 million visitors. A registered charity, the museum's president is Sir Bobby Charlton. Vice Presidents include Sir Alex Ferguson, Sir Trevor Brooking and Sir Geoff Hurst. The Museum's Special Ambassador is Mark Lawrenson. Nationalfootballmuseum.com. @FootballMuseum